HAVE I GOT NEWS FOR YOU

For some obscure reason, the traditions of book publishing dictate that this page should always be left blank – a tradition we are only too happy to uphold.

HAVE I GOT NEWS FOR YOU

Written by Ged Parsons
Compiled by John Ryan
Edited by Richard Wilson
Additional material by Ian Hislop and Paul Merton

EBURY PRESS
LONDON

1 3 5 7 9 10 8 6 4 2

Published in 2006 by Ebury Press, an imprint of Ebury Publishing

Ebury Publishing is a division of the Random House Group

Copyright Hat Trick Productions, 2006
Photographs copyright see page 159

Hat Trick Productions have asserted their right to be identified as
the author of this Work in accordance with the Copyright, Designs
and Patents Act 1988

The Random House Group Limited Reg. No. 954009

Addresses for companies within the Random House Group can be
found at www.randomhouse.co.uk

A CIP catalogue record for this book is available from
the British Library

The Random House Group Limited makes every effort to ensure
that the papers used in our books are made from trees that have
been legally sourced from well-managed and credibly certified
forests. Our paper procurement policy can be found on
www.randomhouse.co.uk

Printed and bound by Clowes in Suffolk

ISBN 00919114248
ISBN (from Jan 2007) 9780091914240

Project Editor: Claire Wedderburn-Maxwell
Designers: Estuary English and Philippa Baile

Is there anyone out there desperate enough to actually have read
this far down? Really?

HOW TO USE THIS BOOK

If you are looking for a detailed, expert, behind-the-scenes guide to the workings of TV's top satirical quiz, then you should have bought the two previous *Have I Got News For You* books years ago, shouldn't you? Those bastards bagged all the good ideas for making a panel game look half-way decent in print. As it is, you're stuck with the 'concept' we eventually came up with. We have just crowbarred a lot of old jokes into loosely assigned categories, with a cursory nod towards alphabetical order.

A FEW MISSING WORDS AT THE START

'ITV DROPS SHOW THAT PITS ██████ AGAINST ████████?'

PAUL MERTON: 'Ant against Dec'.

ROSS NOBLE: 'John Craven against the forces of evil'.

JIMMY CARR (GUEST HOST): The answer is 'elephant against 44 dwarfs'.

PAUL MERTON: Oh, this is the thing where they have 44 dwarfs and can they pull an elephant? Take it to the pictures, give it a few drinks. Cup of coffee later, and a bun.

IAN HISLOP: They're furious when they find out it's an elephant.

PAUL MERTON: Exactly, yeah.

ROSS NOBLE: The elephant's furious when it finds out there's 44 dwarfs? What?! Argh!

PAUL MERTON: Four of 'em, they're all standing on each other's shoulders. With a big coat. 'Hello my dear. What a beautiful trunk you have ...'

JIMMY CARR: Following pressure from animal rights groups, ITV bosses have replaced the controversial programme in the schedules. Viewers will now be able to see a hilarious edition of *You've Been Framed* – the one where the kitten gets caught in a Flymo.

'YOGURT GETS ▮▮▮▮ ?'

PHILL JUPITUS: 'Spelt wrong'.

PAUL MERTON: 'Five O-Levels'.

IAN HISLOP: 'Job in Shadow Cabinet'. The EU has launched one of its period bits of madness. Yoghurt is no longer to be yoghurt, unless it comes from, I think it's Bulgaria. No, this is serious. It's in the constitution, it's got to be a fermented milk-type drink.

ALEXANDER ARMSTRONG (GUEST HOST): That is actually the right answer. 'Yogurt gets culture shock.' This is the news that the EU wants to replace the word 'yogurt' with the phrase: 'mild alternate-culture heat-treated fermented milk.' By the time you've asked for it, your thrush has cleared up all by itself.

AEROPLANES

'THE NEW 380 AIRBUS WILL FEATURE A LOUNGE, A FLATSCREEN WATERFALL AND A LIBRARY.'

The Times

PAUL MERTON: How do you take the books back? Have you got them for three weeks? When you see a plane overhead do you have to throw them back?

SEAN LOCK (GUEST HOST): They're also considering tourist class passengers standing up and leaning against bench seats. But there are drawbacks, according to one plane designer: **'You'd have to make the cabin taller and the backsides of people are in different places, so they would have to be adjustable.'**

PAUL MERTON: What do you mean their backsides are in different places? Excuse me, madam, your bum is behind your ear. Did you pack your arse yourself, sir? We can't find it. Give him somebody else's. That one there, it matches, give him that.

AMBITION

At the National Literacy Awards, the five finalists hand in their essays on 'Why I want to be Prime Minister.'

BORIS JOHNSON
How a host prepares

9.15 Cripes! Wake late — bloody alarm! Hurl clock at wall, only to have it bounce back and hit face. Then discover hadn't actually set alarm — bah! Must arrive at HIGNFY studio by 10 am, so leap straight out of bed. However, also leap straight onto sprog's discarded roller skate. Yaroo! During ensuing painful plummet downstairs, make mental note to repair bannister.

9.21 After brief concussion, wake to find better half and sprogs have left. Hurrah! Will have bathroom all to self. Now to locate it — hmm, tricky one. Ten minutes later, mission accomplished! Miffed to see have bad case of bed-head, i.e. hair is stubbornly neat and tidy. Soon sort it out with prolonged bout of vigorous brushing — with balloon.

9.38 No time for usual 20-minute morning run. Spend next 20 minutes running round, in search of missing shoe, briefcase, manuscript of article on 'Ancient Roman Traffic-Calming', trousers, bicycle clips and other shoe. Grab bite of breakfast and dash out.

9.59 Dash back in for briefcase, dash out again.

10.00 Dash back in for trousers, dash out again.

10.04 Pause during bicycle journey to drop off manuscript — discover it's actually two slices of toast. Realize I've eaten article on 'Ancient Roman Traffic-Calming'.

10.10 Arrive at studio. Phew! Not too late, after all. All know me here, so take short-cut through side entrance.

11.10 Arrive at production office, after finally convincing security staff as to identity. Join producers around table for script meeting.

11.47 Things going well, make copious notes. Crumbs! Suddenly find out it's script meeting for Parkinson. Thought questions were a bit easy. Decide to slip out unnoticed. Knock vase of flowers over tray of coffee and biscuits!

11.49 The working day begins. Meet production team, all good eggs. Splendid! Then informed should have turned up for read-through at company office yesterday — frankly, a bit of a blow. Given 200 pages of script, back-up notes, jokes, gags, quips and assorted funnies, and told to make a start. Crumbs! Thank goodness am blessed with an almost photographic, um, thingummyjig.

12.00 Break for lunch. Good-oh! Absolutely famished! Given directions to studio canteen. Arrive at studio car park. Wander around trying various doors. Arrive back at production office, after finally convincing security staff as to identity. Production team on top form, after large and apparently delicious lunch, including roast beef, spotted dick and custard. Grab limp cheese sandwich and press on.

1.00–3.00 Rehearsal. Acquit self reasonably well, spend two-hour session getting to know Paul, Ian and guests.

Make vast amounts of detailed notes ready for tonight's show. Hurrah! As ever, preparation is all-important! Then informed that these people aren't actually Paul and Ian and guests but, rather, members of production team, just standing-in for rehearsal purposes. Ah, well, live and learn.

3.30 Shown to dressing room. Given impressive sheet of instructions on how to work door code, trouser-press, kettle, washbasin, lavatory, fruit bowl, etc.

5.00 Gosh! Last-minute major news story breaks, about someone famous doing something important, somewhere or other. Given 10 pages of new jokes to read out. Fail to 'get' half of them. Producers thank me, and say those are the ones they'll be using. Have idea for article on 'Ancient Etruscan Dinner Parties'.

5.30 Pre-show buffet. Good-oh! Am absolutely famished. All manner of mouth-watering tuck. Yummy! Nibble olive. Spend next 25 minutes choking on olive stone. Called into make-up. Grab limp cheese sandwich and press on.

6.00 Spend 30 minutes getting dressed and having make-up applied. Very smart, but still not quite right. Then taken outside and dragged backwards through hedge. Perfect!

7.00 Quiet time in dressing room. Dash off article about 'Ancient Greek House Prices'. Absolutely famished. Sympathetic production runner brings cup of vegetable soup.

Tricky blighters, plastic lids. College tie ruined — hopefully, result will be taken for 'floral' design.

7.30 Hurrah! Begin recording show. Twenty-nine minutes of material needed.

9.45 Finish recording show. A few re-takes required. Start to pick up technical TV jargon from production team — all very interesting. Terms like 're-take', 'fluffed line', 'missed cue', 'wrong camera' and 'car-crash'.

10.25 Finish re-takes. Huge cheer from audience, Paul, Ian, guests and entire production team, so must have done OK — hurrah!

10.30 Whisked up to 18th-floor reception room with promise of post-show drinks and nibbles. At last! Am absolutely famished. Waft of delicious aroma. Turns out to be coming from tie. Arrive to find buffet finished — bah! Order celebratory bottle of champagne instead. Propose toast to 'the end of a perfect recording day!' Accidentally pop cork into eye of sympathetic production runner, spray contents over Paul, Ian and guests.

11.00 Say goodbyes and arrive in car park just as producer's limo reverses over bicycle. Crumbs!

CANVASSING

PAUL MERTON: Is it like that film *The Sixth Sense*, when she's suddenly seeing somebody that's dead?

ANDY HAMILTON: Tebbit denies breaking voter's neck in High Street.

PAUL MERTON: New girlfriend raises eyebrows in constituency.

CHARLES KENNEDY

Doctors voice their concern as the press tracks down Charles Kennedy's new PA.

TREVOR McDONALD (GUEST HOST): Who did the dirty on Charles?

LEMBIT OPIK: What a really difficult question. I think that there was a difference of opinion in the party.

TREVOR McDONALD: About what?

IAN HISLOP: About whether he was pissed all the time or not.

MARCUS BRIGSTOCKE: No, they kept him while he was pissed, it was only when he sobered up they decided he's boring and useless. So they got rid of him.

TREVOR McDONALD: The former Liberal Democrat leader Charles Kennedy refused to leave without a fight, which came as no surprise to pub landlords in the Westminster area.

The *Mirror* revealed that one of Charles Kennedy's expense claims included a note to the hotel staff which read: '**Mr Kennedy requires a full set of newspapers by 6.30am.**' Preferably old ones spread out by the side of the bed next to the bucket.

CREDITS

After the famous people have all had their names go by in the end-of-show credits, loads of other people's names appear with important-sounding job titles. But what do they all actually do?

PROGRAMME ASSOCIATES
Write all of the presenter's jokes, which are then rejected or edited out, prior to transmission. They're so bitter that, ironically, no-one else on the programme wants to be associated with them.

SIGNATURE TUNE COMPOSER
Writes a pleasant, catchy tune, and then speeds it up horribly, so it's twice as fast as it should be.

GRAPHICS
Responsible for defacing the studio toilets with obscene diagrams.

MAKE-UP
Performs a vital role whenever there's a shortage of news stories.

COSTUME DESIGNER
Selects clothing to be worn by Paul and Ian. Has best sense of humour on the show.

VISION MIXERS
Sometimes there's just not enough vision in a show, and sometimes there's too much vision. These guys take the vision out, mix it until it's just right, and then put it back.

VIDEOTAPE EDITOR
Knows where the studio scissors are kept.

CAMERA SUPERVISOR
In charge of positioning the six cameras, so has to be able to count up to six.

SOUND SUPERVISOR
A good supervisor in Manchester.

LIGHTING DIRECTOR
Says 'on' and 'off'. Has to change the light bulbs. It only takes one of them.

FLOOR MANAGER
Floor Mopper. Just kidding – their real job is to make sure the audience claps at the right time. Floor Mopper actuallys rank a bit higher.

DESIGN
Creates and constructs the set. Not in fact a drunk monkey with a hammer.

RESEARCHERS
Spend the entire day in search of vital information, i.e. which friends need to be sent e-mails, who drank the most last night, and who's the skinnest celeb in this week's *Heat*.

ASSOCIATE PRODUCERS
Researchers who are good friends of the Producers.

PRODUCTION CO-ORDINATOR
Tells the crew what to wear so they don't clash horribly with each other.

PRODUCTION ACCOUNTANT
Supplies wheelbarrow required to pay Executive Producer.

PRODUCTION TEAM
The two members of the Production Team who think they're the only members of the Production Team who do any work.

PRODUCTION ASSISTANT
Assists the production.

PRODUCTION MANAGER
Er, manages the production.

HEAD OF PRODUCTION
You guessed it.

EXECUTIVE PRODUCTION ADVISOR
This is just taking the piss now, isn't it?

DIRECTOR
Gives the Camera Supervisor a number from one to six.

PRODUCER
Spends the whole show in a corner weeping and gibbering.

SERIES PRODUCER
Spends the whole series in a corner weeping and gibbering.

EXECUTIVE PRODUCER
Fuck knows.

CRIME

In Los Angeles there are new allegations concerning Michael Jackson, as the police receive an anonymous tip-off.

DAVID BLAINE

'BLAINE'S LIFE OR BREATH RESCUE'

In New York, David Blaine failed to break the world record for holding his breath underwater.

As he began to lose consciousness, after more than seven minutes without breathing, he was tragically rescued and brought to the surface.

Doctors apparently warned that David Blaine may be suffering brain damage, but they let him go ahead with the stunt anyway.

David Blaine narrowly failed to beat the previous world record, which was set by a man who held his breath for almost nine minutes, after following John Prescott into the lavatory at the House of Commons.

DAVID BLUNKETT

'Are you mine as well?!'

DES LYNAM
How a host prepares

WEDNESDAY AFTERNOON — a relaxing visit to Alphonse,
my Jermyn Street moustachier. He's been doing me
almost 40 years. Man's a miracle-worker. Nasal massage,
'tache prune, bristle balm — the whole shebang. Full
two-hour session. Calms your nerves, soothes your mind
— marvellous. Peps you up, too, fellas — get my drift?
Glide out refreshed, leaving Alphonse a handsome tip —
hey, it's the only kind I do! Pick up programme script
from TV office, two minutes' speed-reading — little
trick of mine — then on to my health club, The
Perfumed Garden, to unwind with a well-earned
invigorating head rub, courtesy of my personal
trainers, Fifi and Helga.

WEDNESDAY EVENING — a quiet night in. My housemaid
Suki lightly tosses my salad, then it's time to focus
on the task ahead. My secret? Ancient Oriental
meditation. Take my tip, it's just the job. So, it's off
with the old cravat, and into the silk kimono. Dim
lights, soft music. Suki fetches the scented candles and
the soothing oils and, three hours later, I achieve
full nirvana. Spot on! Refreshes your spirit, energizes
your aura — fantastic. Gives you a kick start, too,
fellas — catch my meaning? A last quick exotic
infusion, and then bed.

THURSDAY MORNING — show recording day. Up at 6am, to enjoy 10 minutes' playing with my bamboo flute. Then it's an hour's Tantric stretching with Suki, before I enjoy my usual large early-morning dollop of natural yoghurt. My car arrives, and Marie-Claire, my chauffeuse, whisks me off in style. Studio by 10am, flash my particulars at the charming receptionist, and I'm allowed into her inner sanctum. Production team, mainly lots of lovely girls in their twenties and thirties, seem delighted to see me — amazing what a simple delivery of individual bouquets of wild orchids can do, eh, fellas? Quick talk-through from some chap or other, then I'm off to tell the autocue lady exactly how I'd like her to lay things out for me.

THURSDAY EVENING — show-time. Thanks to a rigorous afternoon session with a couple of assistant researchers, I manage to sail through the recording, and emerge exhausted but happy. Interesting panel — three guys whose names I didn't quite catch, and an intriguing lady journalist. During nibbles afterwards, she gets pretty excited at the thought of me producing my own column. Finally, the production ladies all raise a glass of white wine to me, and I end what's been a perfect evening with a large Semillon. But then, hey! — don't I always?

DIGITAL TELEVISION

Unusually for a show about the week's news, old editions of *Have I Got News For You* are shown many times over, often years after their first transmission. Bad news for original programming but, boy, those repeat fees! Most of the re-runs are on cable and satellite channels, so here is a handy guide for your Sky-Plus machine ...

DIGITAL SCHEDULE

Sky Sports 4

22.00 Ten-Pin Bowling from Coventry Bowlodrome
24.00 Beach Darts – Acapulco Classic
06.30 Giants of Latvian Hockey
08.30 X-treme Angling – Californian Masters
11.00 Have I Got News For You
11.30 International Draughts from Helsinki
18.00 World Cup Free-Style Walking

UK Living Style Plus

10.00 Dry-Lining with Nick Knowles
12.00 Pave It Yourself! with Lowri Turner
13.30 Tool's Gold with Handy Andy
16.00 Lowri's Mouldy Basement with Handy Andy and Nick Knowles
20.00 Have I Got News For You
20.30 Leather Looks with Linda Barker
22.00 Talking Grout with Andy, Lowri, Nick and Linda
03.00 Property, Property, Property, Property

Red Hot Filth UK

09.00 Dirty D**mond's Hot Slutty Shaggers
11.00 Strictly 'Come' Dancing
14.00 Have I Got Ooze For You
16.00 Bare Market – shares update with Jodie Marsh
16.15 A Question of Spurt
18.30 Have I Got News For You
19.00 Rolf's Anal Hospital
19.30 Ready, Steady, Cock!
20.00 Big Cock, Little Cock
20.30 Nigella Bites

Discovering Geographic Channel

09.00 Lost Giant Pygmy Tribes of Africa
10.00 When Sloths Attack
11.00 Lost Pygmy Giant Tribes of Africa
12.00 Mysteries of Sand Erosion: Eastbourne's Youthful OAPs
13.00 Have I Got News For You
13.30 Carnivorous Cacti of Kathmandu
15.00 The World's Wild Places: Sunderland
16.00 Never Mind The Buzzards
17.00 Swaziland's Snail Stampede

Bid-Drop TV

09.00 Pound-Pounder Hour
10.00 Cash-Crasher Hour
11.00 Quid-Quasher Hour
12.00 Dough-Dropper Hour
13.00 Wedge-Whacker Hour
14.00 Bunce-Basher Hour
15.00 Have I Got News For You
15.30 Moolah-Masher Hour
16.30 Spondoolick-Smasher Hour
17.30 Price-Reducing Hour
18.30 Bread-Bruiser Hour
19.30 Price-Reducing Hour

Al-Jeezara

09.00 Talibannies
10.00 Two Fatwah Ladies
11.00 Strictly No Dancing
12.00 Pro-Celebrity Adulterer Stoning
13.00 Have I Got News For You (edit)
13.05 Last of the Summer Water
14.35 Baghdad's Army
15.00 Burka, She Wrote

Males 'n' Motor-cars

22.00 Sleek 'n' Sexy Sports Coupés
22.30 Exotic Estate Cars
23.00 Have I Got News For You
23.30 Steamy Saloons

01.00 Hottest Hatchbacks
01.30 Phwoar x 4 Heaven
02.00 Pertest People-Carriers
02.30 Look! A Real Naked Woman! with Jo Guest

BBC 3

19.00 Two Pints of Lager and a Packet of Crisps
19.30 Two Pints of Lager and a Packet of Crisps
20.00 Two Pints of Lager and a Packet of Crisps
20.30 Two Pints of Lager and a Packet of Crisps
21.00 Omnibus Hour: Two Pints of Lager and a Packet of Crisps

22.00 Two Pints of Lager and a Packet of Crisps
22.30 Have I Got News For You
23.00 Two Pints of Lager and a Packet of Crisps
23.30 Two Pints of Lager and a Packet of Crisps
24.00 Out-Takes: Two Pints of Lager and a Packet of Crisps
00.30 Two Pints of Lager and a Packet of Crisps
01.00 Two Pints of Lager and a Packet of Crisps

BBC News 24

09.00 News
12.00 News
15.00 News
18.00 News

21.00 Have I Got News For You
21.30 News
24.00 News
03.00 News
06.00 News

TV 4 Da Yoof

19.00 LA Kribz In Da Hood
21.00 RnB Flavaz 4 U
22.00 Yo! Itz Da 'Ho To Go!' Sho
23.00 Yo! Itz Mo' 'Ho To Go!' Sho
01.00 Have I Got Newz 4 Yo
01.30 Pimp My Ride
02.00 Ride My Pimp
02.30 LA Hoodz In Da Krib
03.00 Da Hood In Da Thunderbirds

DOCTOR WHO

Regular viewers may be surprised by Paul's revelation that Ian is to be the next Doctor Who. We have obtained the storyboard for the opening episode of the new series to be shown next spring...

33

DODGY PEERAGES

Labour are expected to launch their own independent enquiry into dodgy peerages ...

Even more interestingly, it's to be led by Lord Levy, Lord Goldsmith and Lord Falconer. And if you don't want to know the result, bury your head in your hands now.

In the wake of the scandal, Labour are reviewing their loan policy, the Tories have returned millions of pounds to their backers and the Lib Dem's top donor has got his book token back.

DONEGAN

Skiffle pioneer, Lonnie Donegan died in 2002. Mark Knopfler and Rolf Harris played at his tribute show. Friends say it's what he would have wanted - to be dead at the time.

DONKEY

GYLES BRANDRETH (GUEST HOST): Just before we go, there's time for the Caption Competition. Paul and Carol, get this.

CAROL SMILLIE: What is it, a piece of ass, Santa?

PAUL MERTON: Is the man on the right saying, 'You're not the woman I married'? Or is the one on the left saying to the man on the right, 'Is it just me, or are those donkey's ears like two Cornish pasties?'

GYLES BRANDRETH: Very good. Thank you.

PAUL MERTON: Thank you.

GYLES BRANDRETH: Thank you.

CAROL SMILLIE: You're very welcome.

PAUL MERTON: No, thank you.

GYLES BRANDRETH: Thank you.

PAUL MERTON: No, thank you.

GYLES BRANDRETH: No, thank you.

PAUL MERTON: I insist.

GYLES BRANDRETH: Fuck off!

PAUL MERTON: He goes off people quickly, doesn't he, old Tommy Two-Ways?

GYLES BRANDRETH: Ah, if I were Tommy Three-Ways, you'd be in with a chance.

PAUL MERTON: If you were Tommy-Two-Thousand-Ways, I wouldn't be in with a chance. Oh, I don't know though, it is Christmas.

DOPPELGANGER

In Westminster, there is a clear winner in the Cherie
Blair look-a-like contest.

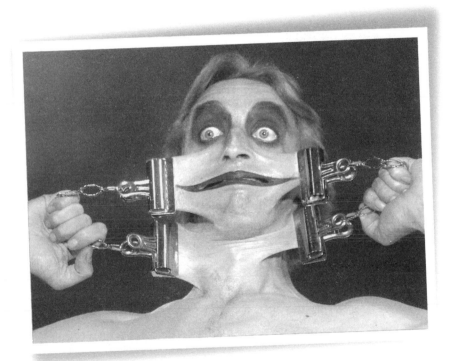

E

eBAY

> 'For sale on eBay: a collection of my cheating wife's knickers.'

ALEXANDER ARMSTRONG (GUEST HOST): A Shropshire man put his cheating wife's knickers up for sale on eBay.

According to the *Express*: **'You will often be surprised by how much you can get for things you think are worthless.'** But not always.

This signed photo of Ian Hislop, for example, has a reserve price of 99 pence, and has so far attracted no bids. You might be interested to know, Ian, that, as of yesterday, the site had only received six hits. But you must bear in mind that four of those are from researchers on this programme.

One week later ...

DARA O'BRIAIN (GUEST HOST): What other art has gone up in value immensely in the last week?

PAUL MERTON: I'm not going to tell you.

DARA O'BRIAIN: It is a picture of Ian Hislop.

IAN HISLOP: Oh, this isn't this eBay thing, is it?

DARA O'BRIAIN: Yes, it is this eBay thing.

Last week, when featured on the show, the signed photograph of Ian Hislop was going for 99 pence. The close price at the end of the auction was £113.11.

IAN HISLOP: That's sick.

JULIA HARTLEY-BREWER: Have you noticed though, even in that picture he's a little bit too short for the photo booth?

DARA O'BRIAIN: There were higher bids. The bids at one stage reached 10 million pounds. The auction was originally done to raise money for a primary school building, and one poor woman was up all night dealing with fake eBay bids. Finally she was so annoyed, she actually wrote in to *Have I Got News For You* to complain about the show invading her privacy, and I have to say I agree. If you agree with me as well and you want to send her a message of support, her e-mail address is Julierose45@hotmail.com.

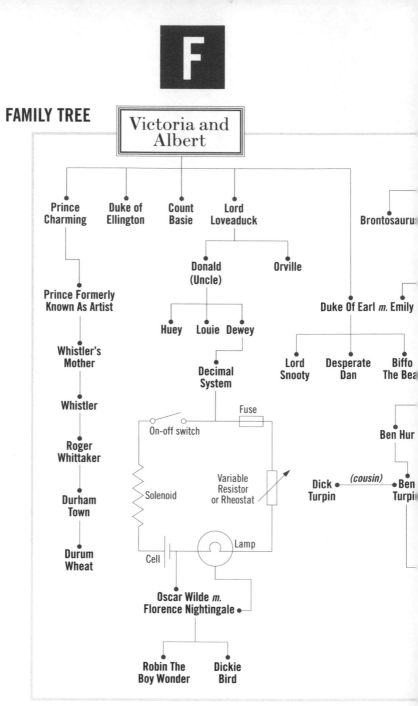

F

FAMILY TREE

Victoria and Albert

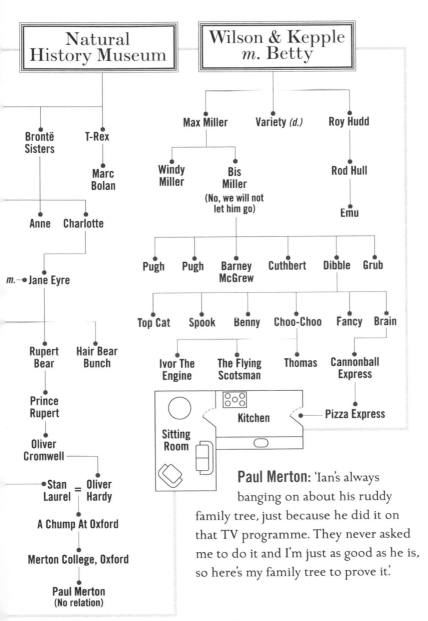

Natural History Museum

Wilson & Kepple
m. Betty

Brontë Sisters

T-Rex

Marc Bolan

Anne   Charlotte

m.—• Jane Eyre

Rupert Bear   Hair Bear Bunch

Prince Rupert

Oliver Cromwell

•Stan Laurel = Oliver Hardy

A Chump At Oxford

Merton College, Oxford

Paul Merton
(No relation)

Max Miller   Variety *(d.)*   Roy Hudd

Windy Miller   Bis Miller
(No, we will not let him go)

Rod Hull

Emu

Pugh   Pugh   Barney McGrew   Cuthbert   Dibble   Grub

Top Cat   Spook   Benny   Choo-Choo   Fancy   Brain

Ivor The Engine   The Flying Scotsman   Thomas   Cannonball Express

Kitchen

Sitting Room

Pizza Express

Paul Merton: 'Ian's always banging on about his ruddy family tree, just because he did it on that TV programme. They never asked me to do it and I'm just as good as he is, so here's my family tree to prove it.'

FESTIVALS

At a pre-dawn drugs bust in Glastonbury,
Boris Johnson pleads his ignorance.

FREEDOM OF SPEECH

After a commotion at the Labour Conference, party officials confirm that the heckling pensioner's complaint has been dealt with.

GAMBLING

At Kempton Park, after blowing the day's winnings on the last race, it's a long walk home for one unlucky punter.

GENETIC MODIFICATION

People often ask why there hasn't been a permanent host on *HIGNFY* for the past four years, to which the obvious answer is 'Yeah, whatever.' Actually, it's not as easy as you might think to find one person who embodies all the different skills and attributes required to sit in a chair and read jokes out. If only we could take the best bits of our guest presenters and combine them. Like this...

Another random combination of unrelated physical features produces this result ...

GROUTING

Long-suffering fans of *Have I Got News For You* may remember that one feature of the show 'Before The Reshuffle' was the convoluted way the then-host referred to the scores, the winners of the show and even the entirely imaginary prizes they had won. Here's an example: **'This week's pinheads are Ian and David with six points, while this week's eggheads are Paul and Janet with 13.'**

The programme's writers who were prevailed upon to come up with these peculiar turns of phrase refer them as 'grouting', i.e. no more than unexciting 'filler'. Anyone who laments the passing of 'grouting' will no doubt enjoy these classics from the archives ...

SCORES AT THE END OF ROUND ONE

(The score at the end of Round One is always tied – it is always four-all or two-all).

'The scores are as even as Stevens can be, being as they are, four-all.'

'The score situation is rather like Baghdad city centre – completely level – at four points each.'

'Unlike [insert piss-head *du jour*], the scores are perfectly balanced at four-all.'

'The scores are like the legs on a Sellafield sheep – four each side.'

'... all of which final respects mark the demise of this past round, and the grim news is that both teams are dead level on four.'

'At the end of that round, the scores are as different as chalk and chalk, both sides having four points.'

'And the pegging has never been so level, with both teams on four.'

'At the end of that round, one two has two twos, the other two has two twos, too.' *(Yes, really.)*

LATER ON, WHEN THE SCORES ARE DIFFERENT

(*i.e. Paul is winning*)

'... all of which musical travesties act as a cataclysmic finale to this penultimate round, and the score is: Ian and John have a rather "bass" six, while Paul and Graham are two short of a "tenor" with eight.'

'... all of which neutral tones call this odd round to account and, on current evidence, Ian and Margaret are in the red with five, while Paul and Brad are in the pink with 13.'

'... all of which undue care and attention brings us skidding to the end of this cul-de-sac, and Ian and Mahatma are trailing with five, while Paul and Mikhail are blazing ahead with eight.'

'... all of which animated discussion leaves us literally speechless, with Ian and Benazir looking dumb and dumber, trailing as they are, five to seven.'

'... all of which party animal behaviour marks the end of this session, and the situation is that Ian and Queen Isabella are swiftly losing their deposit with five, whilst Paul and Alvin have a right honourable six.'

INTRODUCING THE ODD ONE OUT ROUND

'This being our last show of the series, we thought we'd make it our Odd One Out round, so that it conformed to every other show we've ever done.'

'"Let's have another round" – as (insert piss-head *du jour*) would say. Odd One Out is the usual tipple.'

'The Odd One Out round is next, where even a monkey has a one in four chance of getting it right, so let's see how he does – Paul ...'

'Round Seven ... doesn't exist. So let's concentrate instead on Round Three – our quarterly Odd One Out round.'

'So, two rounds down and just 32 to go before the end of the series, as we enter the Odd One Out round.'

LOSERS AND WINNERS

'This week's prize turkeys are Ian and Peter with eight, while this week's proud cocks are Paul and Sarah with 14.'

'This week's dog's breakfasts are Ian and Natalie with six, while this week's dog's bollocks are Paul and Luke with 11.'

'This week's smackheads are Ian and Lemmy with 11, while this week's eggheads are Paul and Giles with 12.'

'This weeks cock-ups ... this week's pin-ups ...'

'This week's black holes ... this week's supernovas ...'

'This week's flash-in-the-pans ... this week's bright sparks ...' (*Getting a bit strained, aren't they?*)

'This week's bloomers ... this week's smarty-pants ...'

PRIZES

(*There aren't any*)

'So, hats off to our winners, piss off to our losers.'

'Congratulations to our winners, the rest of Cliff Richard's records to our losers.'

'The best of British to our winners, *The Best of Val Doonican* to our losers.' (*You can tell that the writers found these a lot easier to do.*)

'Twenty-five pounds' worth of Tesco's vouchers to our winners, the rest of Channel Five's budget to our losers.'

'A photo signed by the Duchess of York to our winners, a cheque signed by the Duchess of York to our losers.'

'A shiny new apple to our winners, a dodgy old Amstrad to our losers.'

'A snort of derision to our losers, a snort of best Colombian to our winners.'

'A walk in the park with George Michael to our winners, a chance to retype that sentence without the spelling mistake to our losers.'

'ELECTION SPECIAL', VERSION OF THE SAME JOKE

'So, to our winners, a chance to go to Michael Portillo's constituency to see the count. To our losers, a chance to retype that sentence without the spelling mistake.'

GUEST PUBLICATIONS

Have I Got News For You has used so many guest publications over the years that there is a serious risk that the world will one day run out of these valuable communication tools. We need your help to find new titles. Select a word at random from each column of our Guest Publication Name Generator to create a brand-new publication.

If you come up with a really dull one and have no other joy in your life, why not actually publish it yourself and send it to us?

CROCODILE	GROWERS'	JOURNAL
BUNION	MARKETING	TIMES
ORGAN	RECYCLING	REVIEW
GRAVEL	LOVERS'	SOLUTIONS
NUDE	POLISHING	ILLUSTRATED
SEWAGE	SWAPPERS'	MANAGEMENT
HAMSTERS	HAMSTERS	HAMSTERS
POTATO	SOLVENT	INTERNATIONAL
GOOD	WELDING	TODAY

CATTLE	SHREDDER	DIGEST
MURDERING	BALLAST	WEEKLY
AMATEUR	OSTLER	FOR BEGINNERS
ADVANCED	PIGEON	MACHINIST
ELECTRIC	MIND	STORIES
WOGAN	AVIONICS	PROGRAMMER
MODEL	DOG	ECHO
VINTAGE	LUBRICATION	WORLD
NATURAL	FINANCE	PEOPLE
PYJAMA	GIZMO	ABSTRACTS
TROPICAL	TROUSER	PRESS
ORGANIC	SPOTTERS'	UPDATE
PUZZLE	RESTORING	MADE SIMPLE
VIRTUAL	SOFT TOY	ADVERTISER
TRUE	PLATE-COLLECTING	EXPLAINED

H

HEAT

Unlike *Have I Got News For You*, which presents objective comment and reasoned analysis to its well-informed viewers, *heat* magazine purveys salacious gossip and cheap tittle-tattle to its gullible readership. It also takes great pleasure in highlighting the slightest physical imperfections in the bodies of celebrities whom its, no doubt superbly-proportioned reporters, can't wait to make fun of. Here are a few *heat* items you may have missed.

We bet Jordan wishes she'd brought her rubber gloves to this swish awards ceremony, after she was spotted with wrinkly hands! She's obviously mislaid the airbrush. Or maybe we have? Who knows? Hands up who's got wrinkly hands? We say, 'Haven't you heard of Nivea, Katie?'

spotted!

- **Davina McCall** gurning like a Macaque monkey on national television
- **Dale Winton** supervising a concrete-pour on the Beckton Flyover
- **Jeremy Kyle** in the crosshairs of a mystery sniper's rifle which jams at the crucial moment, dammit
- **Jeffrey Archer** at the Royal Opera House, trying to get backstage claiming to be Pavarotti's brother

- an engrossed **Will Self** in Bracknell Waterstone's, leafing through a Maeve Binchy
- **Bruce Forsyth** dancing an 'in-your-face' jig in Hyde Park, after beating his grandson at crazy golf
- *NOTW* editor, **Rebekah Wade**, in Battersea, coming out of a kick-boxing class
- **Ross Kemp**, in Battersea, nursing a broken arm
- **Jeremy Paxman** at White City tube station, repeatedly asking a guard when the next train is

- **Robert Kilroy Silk** in Knightsbridge, eating a falafel
- **Piers Morgan** being asked to take part in numerous TV shows by shameless BBC executives
- **David Frost** on a Chardonnay drip
- **Menzies Campbell** in Fortnum and Mason's, buying a tartan blanket and a jar of mint humbugs
- **John Prescott** in Hull, carrying a sleeping bag out to the garage
- An olive-skinned man of Middle-Eastern appearance, who looks a bit like a known terrorist

suspect, running along – oh hang on, lost him
- **Sir Ian Blair**, in a shopping precinct, doing wheelies on his bike
- **Paul Merton** and a boater-wearing friend, queuing for croquet tickets at the Hurlingham Club
- **George Galloway** making a surprise visit to the House of Commons
- a smiling **Prince Edward** carrying quite clearly someone else's feather boa outside Madame Jo-Jo's in Soho

- **David Cameron**, helping a beggar across the road, jogging to his evening shift at the Samaritans, downloading some cool tracks to his iPod Nano, and snowboarding with the Arctic Monkeys
- **Michael Parkinson** fawning over anyone vaguely famous
- **Sir Elton John** buying a tin of own-brand spaghetti hoops from the Walthamstow branch of Netto (unconfirmed)
- **Tony Blair** busking at Marble Arch tube station
- **Ian Hislop** enjoying a half-time burger at Millwall vs. Cardiff City at The New Den, Bermondsey
- **Boris Johnson** Publishing old columns under the title of a well-known topical news quiz.
- **Tessa Jowell** in Kentish Town, choosing a ready-meal for one at M&S

- **Jeremy Clarkson** walking
- **Eddie Izzard** in Ealing High Street, looking in Millet's window

Posh's hair

Urrgh she sometimes goes to the toilet, you know.

- **Darren Day** stocking up on engagement rings at Argos
- **David Blunkett** in Annabel's disco, chatting to a hat stand
- **Sir Alan Sugar** selling speakers from a white van

- **Prince Philip** in his cab, arguing with a Chinese tourist at Heathrow
- an emotional **William Hague** in the Red Lion pub in Westminster, being asked to leave after his second pint

- **Chris Evans** at the BBC, being unable to believe his luck
- **Jamie Oliver** and family, going large in Maidstone McDonald's
- **Lord Deedes** trying to overpower Eamonn Holmes with chloroform
- **Jodie Marsh** in the Egyptology section at the British Library
- Former U.N. **Secretary-General Perez De Cuellar** cutting keys in a heel bar in Leeds
- **Mylene Klass** winning the British Open ping-pong championship
- **Gordon Brown** cancelling an appointment at the Westminster branch of Pickford's
- **Angus Deayton** on ITV, presenting some programme or other

HEIST

At the Tower of London, security guards foil a
smash-and-grab raid by a desperate intruder.

HERALDRY

In 2005, as a result of a drunken nine-hour game of poker at Prince Charles' second stag-night party, the show was granted its own coat-of-arms.

Here, one of the Kings of Arms, the senior heralds of the College of Arms, explains the significance of the symbolism behind this proud emblem.

As is traditional, the central shield is flanked by two supporters. To the left, a bull is surmounted by a cock, the pair representing the nature of many news stories. To the right, a winged boar symbolizes the programme's usual response when faced with politicians' promises, public service pledges and the like.

The central shield is quartered, and features symbols which relate to several familiar elements in the programme. The Wheel corresponds to the renowned Wheel of News feature; the Book stands for the Missing Words round; the Sun on its side refers to knocking the tabloids; and the pair of Jaguars recalls the Rt Hon. John Prescott, MP.

The programme's attacks on favourite figures of ridicule, such as Mr Prescott, Mr Kilroy Silk and Lord Archer are symbolized by the shooting of a fish in a barrel.

The design is completed with a Latin motto.

❧

If you're someone who doesn't like heraldry – and let's face it, that's most of us – you could use the coat-of-arms as a fun puzzle instead. Our artist got understandably bored, and included four tiny pictures of a bicycle, a pineapple, a Smiley and a gun in his drawing. Can you find them?

HOME OFFICE

ANDY HAMILTON: I thought Blair was very naïve, because he got up and he said, 'of course there are no figures for the number of illegal immigrants in this country, because by definition they are illegal, therefore there's no official number. And I thought, well, in that case, just make one up.

ALEXANDER ARMSTRONG (GUEST HOST): Yes.

ANDY HAMILTON: If Cameron says, 'how many illegal immigrants are there in the country?' You say, '7,412, sit down'. If he says, 'I don't believe you', say, 'all right, 11'.

FERN BRITTON: They found five in the Home Office working as cleaners.

IAN HISLOP: Yeah. Cleaners of the desks of people who are there to enforce the asylum law.

PHIL HAMMOND: John Reid kept asking questions about where all the illegal immigrants are, even though I can tell you, they're working in the NHS. We've got this huge organization, you could be a locum in the NHS for years without fear of detection. As I was saying to Dr Bin Laden only the other day ...

ALEXANDER ARMSTRONG: Yes, it's the new broom sweeping through the Home Office.

Unfortunately, the broom's being held by a cleaner, who's an illegal immigrant from Somalia.

The Home Office admits it will take over a hundred years to systematically sort through the backlog of files concerning asylum seekers. So, if you're watching, Mr Zebedee Zachariah from Zanzibar, you're probably safe for a while.

INNOVATION

At a trade fair in Tokyo, a potential investor is delighted to meet James Dyson's wife.

IRAQ

In Baghdad, there's evidence at last that the Iraqis do possess dangerous chemical weapons.

JEREMY CLARKSON
How a host prepares

WEDNESDAY, LATE AFTERNOON.

A busy recording day always takes it out of you, so
it's only common sense to prepare for these things
properly. After dropping by the office to pick up the
script, which the producers have somehow convinced
themselves I'm actually going to bother reading,

I head off to my favourite high-octane North London
curry house, the E-Type Sag, to ensure I'm adequately
fuelled-up for the challenge ahead. I plump for my
usual order — the Special Wild Game Balti Banquet for
One, a man-pleasing combination of pungent Indian
spices and endangered British wildlife: Otter Phal,
Vole Vindaloo, Fieldmouse Dhansak and Badger Bhaji. We
have ignition! (Must let AA Gill know about this.)

WEDNESDAY, NIGHT.

Before a show, I personally find there's no better way to relax than by frantically playing some high-tech computer race-game. Oh, yes! After surveying the options, I select Formula One's formidable Jenson Button to be my opponent, and then I'm off — hurtling at breakneck speed around a fun course that snakes its way treacherously through the crowded streets of central London. After half-an-hour of white-knuckle kick-ass thrills, Jenson and I finally arrive at my house, where I park noisily, and the two of us rush inside to start playing on the console. Brilliant fun! Just time to check the sales figures for my anthology of car number-plates — sitting nicely atop the paperback non-fiction/TV spin-off/recycled newspaper columns best-seller chart for the 28th week. Bingo!

THURSDAY, EARLY MORNING.

These days, I find I'm needing at least eight hours — but that long counting money doesn't leave you with much time for sleep. As a result, my better half needs to serve me up a proper, full cooked breakfast to get me going. Disappointingly, she's taken her eye off the ball for once, and the coffee turns out to be French, but it's nothing a good, old-fashioned dollop of English mustard can't solve. Bring it on! Suitably refreshed, I discover I'm running late. Utter mayhem ensues! I then fritter away another five seconds deciding what to wear, throw on a jacket and jeans, and set off on the 40-mile drive to the studio.

THURSDAY MORNING, LATER.

Typical! Absolutely bloody typical! Why does this always, always, always happen when you're in a hurry to get somewhere?

I eventually arrive, hot and flustered, after a completely horrendous and frustrating eight-minute journey from hell Grrr! Still, I cheer up a bit after I install a new ringtone for my phone. It's one I recorded myself while test-driving armoured personnel carriers for Top Gear recently — the catchy, distinctive double-thump of a large squirrel being reversed over, followed by a high-pitched girlie yelp from a horrified Richard Hammond. Ace!

THURSDAY AFTERNOON.

Ho-hum. During yet another one of those interminable TV technical delays, when everyone's hanging around doing nothing in particular, I seize the chance to nip out to the studio loo for five minutes and knock out 1000 words for The Sunday Times on good old-fashioned Bronco paper, versus poofy Andrex. Ker-ching! Disturbed by loud theme music and knocking on door ... OK, let's roll!

JOHN PRESCOTT

JULIAN CLARY (GUEST HOST): There was embarrassment for John Prescott after allegations that he and his secretary Tracey Temple had sex in his office with the door open. Mainly so he could listen out for the pizza delivery boy.

PAUL MERTON: Thin and crusty?

JULIAN CLARY: Tracey Temple's new celebrity status means she has now been offered the opportunity to appear on *Love Island*. Although, from what I've seen, she's already spent two years on him.

The *Mirror* revealed: **'At a Christmas party, he gathered her up in his arms and twirled her round in the air.'**

Serves her right, pushing in front of him in the buffet queue.

The affair started over a romantic dinner, with Prescott whispering sweet nothings: **'I love you sausage, you're my little dumpling. Oh, hello luv. Sorry, I started without you.'**

In the last election a total of £75,000 was spent upgrading John Prescott's battle bus, by adding a waterbed, mirrors on the ceiling and strengthening the rear suspension.

THERE'S MORE...

MARK STEELE: I'm hoping that he doesn't get sacked over this, because if he does, it's a farce. It will mean that it's all right to be Deputy Leader of a government that takes the country into an illegal war, but shag your secretary and have a game of croquet and that's beyond the pale. I think it would be like if Fred West had been jailed, but for not paying VAT on the cement.

JULIAN CLARY: Some of Prescott's friends have been leaping to his defence. One of his ex-advisers said: **'Mr Prescott is a workaholic, working 16 hours a day, seven days a week.'** Two weeks a year.

One of John Prescott's colleagues told the newspapers: **'Tuesday Mr Prescott was co-ordinating the government's response to the Indonesian earthquake.'**

They told him not to jump off the chair again.

JUMP

At Blackpool Tower, there's yet another failed suicide attempt for Britain's unluckiest man.

K

KNOCK, KNOCK
Who's there?
Some jokes that wouldn't fit anywhere else.

Ian McKellen is available in unofficial Lego as Gandalf. As a result of the *Lord of the Rings* movies, more and more children are picking up the original Tolkien books and saying, 'Blimey, a thousand pages, you're having a laugh, I'm not reading that!'

Simon Hughes' manifesto for his campaign to become London Mayor offered a number of promises on public transport, including:
'An end to three buses all at once.'
I don't know, you wait ages for a manifesto promise and then it's a crap one.

Liz Hurley starred in a film version of *Samson and Delilah*, in which every ounce of Samson's strength is drained from his body as he watches Hurley trying to act.

It was Alastair Campbell who famously spotted that John Major tucked his shirt into his underpants after coming out of a toilet on a plane, though the scoop he missed was that Edwina was still in there straightening her skirt.

One female journalist having lunch with meat enthusiast Hugh Fearnley-Whittingstall admitted she felt squeamish when presented with 'an entire tongue, grey and curled fatly around on itself like a question mark' – which Hugh now admits was a bit forward for a first date.

After being found guilty of helping Major Ingram cheat on *Who Wants To Be A Millionaire*, Tequin Whittock was threatened with prison, where he'd have no doubt discovered a different meaning to the expression 'fastest finger first'.

Richard Curtis created the film *Love Actually* in which the Prime Minister falls in love with the Downing Street tea lady back in 1982. Which is when Margaret Thatcher was Prime Minister. So, some sort of lesbian horror movie there.

LAW ENFORCEMENT

WILL SELF: 'There's hardly any point in putting our sirens on in this situation. Oh let's put them on anyway.'

IAN HISLOP: 'Where did you say that Brazilian bloke was?'

LORDI

CAROL VORDERMAN (GUEST HOST): Lordi has a rock 'n' roll motto. Anyone know what it is?

PAUL MERTON: 'We don't believe in Clearasil'.

CAROL VORDERMAN: 'Europe Get Ready to Get Scared.' Didn't Bucks Fizz use that? Or was it Hitler?

PAUL MERTON: There is always a confusion between Hitler and Bucks Fizz, yes. Traditionally over the years.

PHIL HAMMOND: When you draw the Venn diagram, there's a bit of overlap in the middle isn't there?

PAUL MERTON: Exactly. And just before he invaded Poland he was hesitating and somebody said, 'What's that?' He said, 'I'm Just Making My Mind Up'.

LYRICS

The producers of the show realized that a simple, catchy theme tune is essential to the success of any TV programme. But they still went ahead with the theme you can hear to this very day. What you might not know is that there are lyrics to go with this 'tune'.

Next time the show is on, why not try to sing along? Good luck!

Most shows have a tune that's pretty easy to sing, but
This one's rotten – we'd forgotten
Which composer we had to ring.
The tempo's rapid, the words are vapid
And they don't mean a thing.

You can try as you might, but it'll never sound right.
You can do what you can, but still the damn thing won't scan.
You can start high or low – but, no, the bastard won't flow.
And then it all goes down like this ...

'Cos, as you feared ...
It's really weird.
And-then-it-all-stops-quite-abruptly-like-this!

AVE I GOT NEWS FOR YOU

SIC BY BIG GEORGE WEBLEY

© Big George 1990

MEMORY

On a shopping trip to Harrods, there are worries that the Queen is becoming forgetful in her old age.

On her 80th birthday, the Queen received many presents from members of her family. Prince Philip gave her jewellery, Princess Anne gave her chocolates and Prince Charles booked her a week's sky-diving in Iraq.

MERCHANDISE

If you're such a fan of the show that you're actually enjoying reading all this, then you'll just love all the other items of topical-current-affairs-based-panel-show-inspired merchandise that are now available, brought to you direct from the House of *HIGNFY*.

TRANSFORM YOUR HOME WITH THESE OFFICIAL
HAVE I GOT NEWS FOR YOU CURTAINS!

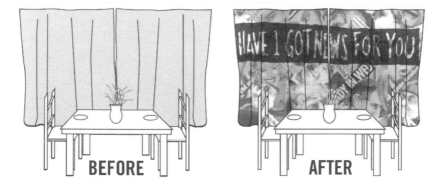

BEFORE   **AFTER**

Yes, imagine the sheer pleasure of being able to turn any room in your home into a stunning replica of the world-famous *HIGNFY* set. Now it's oh-so-easy, thanks to these wonderfully elegant curtains, spun from 100% Nylonette by the renowned master weavers of Gdansk. Printed with the show's distinctive logo, these delightful drapes will bring a sophisticated air of jaded political critique to your lounge, dining room, bedroom, guest room, or just about anywhere! (Non-washable, highly flammable.)

Red and Black
£399.99 per pair

GUEST HOST RONNIE CORBETT SAYS, 'AT LAST! WATCH YOUR FAVOURITE SHOW IN COSY COMFORT! SIT UP, AND BANISH AWKWARD "SATIRE-SLOUCH" FOREVER!'

Now you can own the very same style of cushion as perched upon by loveable little Ronnie C. when he guest hosted the show. Covered in genuine plush-feel Statikon fabric, this enchanting cushion is hand-stuffed by the famed haberdashers of Krakow. If the 'missing word' in your life is 'luxury', then you simply must buy this authentic Ronnie Corbett Guest Host Cushion now!

Red and Black, 18" square x 16" high
£49.99

MAKE EVERY MEALTIME A 'FEAST' OF LAUGHTER WITH THIS OFFICIAL *HAVE I GOT NEWS FOR YOU* UNIQUE 'PAUL 'N' IAN' SALT 'N' PEPPER SET

Your guests will think you're totally condi-mental when you serve up this crazy cruet set at your next dinner party. They'll gasp at the uncannily lifelike appearance of these miniature, seasoning-filled busts of your favourite topical TV team captains. Each incredibly detailed yet culinarily practical head is delicately captured, and cast in solid Steelium by the fabled Jewelsmiths' Guild of Lodz. 'Salt-of-the-earth' funny-man Paul is the perfect choice for the salt cellar, while the peppery wit of Ian makes him the ideal pepper pot.

'Seasons any dish ... allegedly!'
Silver-ish-like, 4"
£99.99 per pair

IT'S USEFUL, IT'S DECORATIVE, IT'S EDUCATIONAL, IT'S FUN!

Do you wish you were a little more interesting and a little more charismatic? If so, then you need this – the only Official *Have I Got News For You* 'Odd One Out' Wall Mirror.

How does it work? Simple. Each frame – carved in solid Oaklene by the skilled craftschildren of Katowice – contains four panels, three of which are designed to hold interchangeable pictures of famous faces. The fourth panel is an ordinary everyday mirror. Just hang up the frame, slot in the pictures of your choice from the range supplied, then look at yourself in the mirror. Hey, presto! – you're now part of your very own Odd One Out round!

How interesting does that make you feel? You'll be the envy of your friends, as they try to work out what you could possibly have in common – or not – with the likes of Joan of Arc, Groucho Marx and Wayne Rooney! Hours of fun.

Red and Black. Includes starter pack of three pictures
£49.99

MISSING WORDS

JACK DEE (GUEST HOST): Missing Words is the final round, featuring the guest publication, *Clay Times*, which carries the strapline: 'Clay Builds Characters'. And here is one of the characters you can build.

'GERSTLEY BORATE IS TO BE ▬▬?'

PAUL MERTON: Is it 'New Clay King of East Sussex'?

IAN HISLOP: Is it 'Potter of the Year'?

JACK DEE: He's not a person, Gerstley Borate. It's to be 'discontinued'.

PAUL MERTON: Oh, I've just bought shares.

JACK DEE: It's actually an additive for pottery glaze, in case you were wondering. The manufacturers have promised: **'We have enough supplies of Gerstley Borate to last for a year, unless there's a run on it.'** So please, please, hold the panic buying, for God's sake, just buy what you need.

'CAMPBELL: MY WORK IS ABOUT ▆▆▆▆▆ ?'

PAUL MERTON: 'Condensing soup'. 'My work is about condensing soup'. There is a company now that sells tins of water which you add soup to.

CLARE BALDING: 'My work is about finished'.

JACK DEE: It probably is right if we were talking about that Campbell, but we're not.

PAUL MERTON: 'Stuffing mincemeat into gnome's mouths'.

JACK DEE: Wrong again. 'My work is about spontaneity'. This is from *Clay Times* and that was Barb Campbell, creator of such classic clay masterpieces as this:

And then she went to big school.

MORE LATE NEWS

PAUL MERTON: Fifty-four days in, magic gnome still pissing.

IAN HISLOP: Iain Duncan Smith makes a comeback?

PAUL MERTON: Remember, do not return to Iain Duncan Smith until you're entirely sure he is out.

NEIL KINNOCK
How a host prepares

NEWS 24

FERN BRITTON: News 24 were doing an item on the internet and someone at the BBC thought this Nigerian bloke was an IT expert, but I think he was there for a job interview wasn't he?

IAN HISLOP: He'd come for a job interview for Director General.

ALEXANDER ARMSTRONG (GUEST HOST): No, it was for the post of IT Assistant. Or as the BBC described it: 'Data support cleanser.'

ANDY HAMILTON: When the story first broke they said he was a taxi driver, didn't they. But when you actually saw the TV interview, you thought, no, he can't be a taxi driver, because a taxi driver would talk more authoritatively about something he knew nothing about. And he'd have done it with his back to her as well, wouldn't he. 'Don't talk to me about Apple, oh well, I had one once.'

PAUL MERTON: To be fair, I did read he's only learnt English in the last four years.

ALEXANDER ARMSTRONG: He taught himself English.

IAN HISLOP: He also taught Prescott English.

ANDY HAMILTON: I know for a fact that's not the first time the BBC have done that. But usually they hush it up. Huw Edwards came to deliver pizza in 1987 and they've kept him on as newsreader, because they don't want to draw attention to the mistake.

PAUL MERTON: No, exactly. But if his phone rings half-way through, he's got to go on his moped and he's out.

NEWS IN BRIEFS

With no apologies to *The Sun*

RICHARD, 56, FROM NECKER

Richard is appalled at the deteriorating situation in Iraq. He said: 'It's dreadful. With the dire shortage of housing, hospitals and schools, there's hardly any need for exciting new Megastore record shops.'

MICHAEL, 71, FROM BARBADOS

Michael is concerned about the poor nutritional value of school dinners. He said: 'Where's Cesare? This isn't my usual table. Don't you know who I am?'

To get this picture on your mobile, simply text **NOSEBAG to 08081571**

WAYNE, 20, FROM LIVERPOOL

Wayne is delighted that nuclear fusion could become a viable energy source. He said: 'The news that plasma scientists have discovered a way to prevent super-hot gases from causing damage within reactors, is mint, la'.'

To get this picture on your mobile, simply text **LUMMOX to 08081571**

CLIFF, 79, FROM PORTUGAL

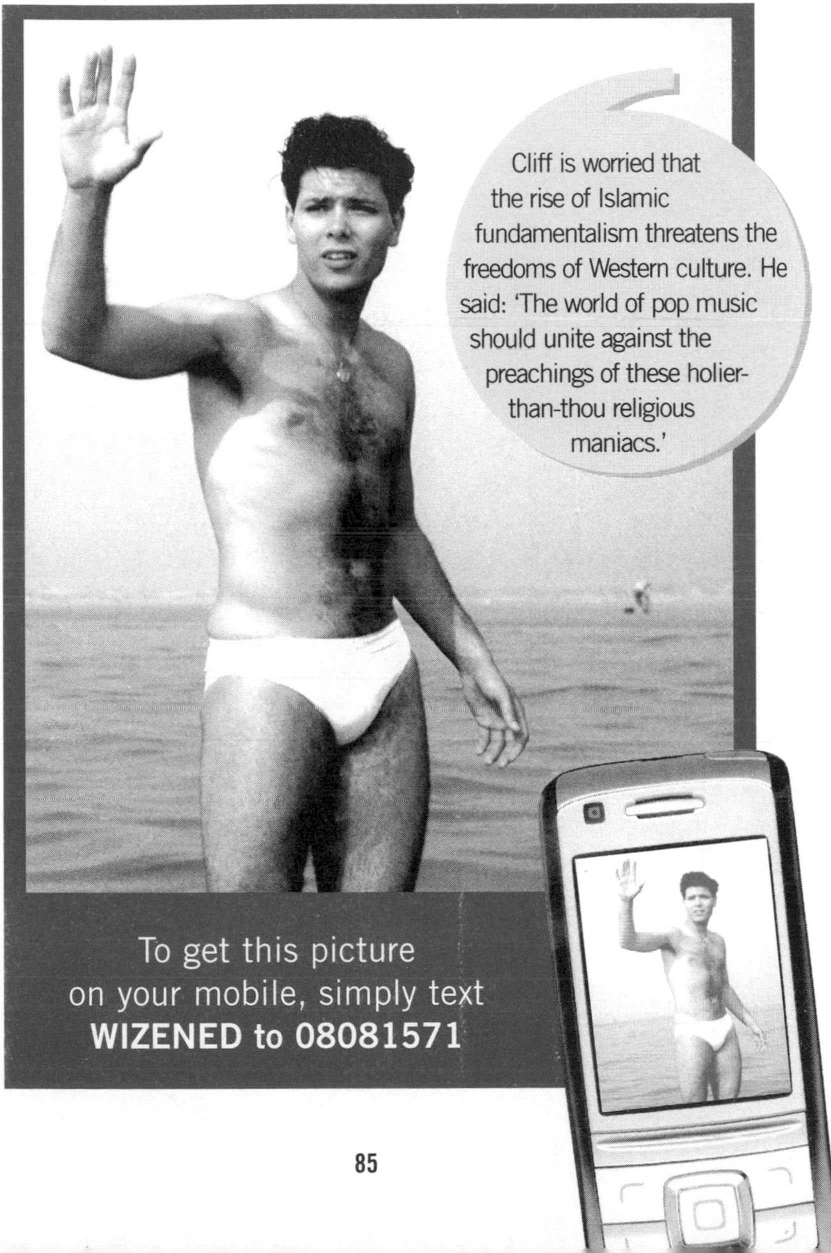

MADONNA, 48, FROM AMERICA

To get this picture on your mobile, simply text **MUTTON to 08081571**

NHS

Health Secretary Patricia Hewitt was booed at a nurses' conference after claiming the NHS has had its best year ever. She says: **'We have written a very big cheque for the NHS.'**

And a delighted GP in the Shetlands is cashing it in as we speak.

The news that NHS doctors earn a quarter of a million pounds a year has shocked many people, not least private doctors, who can't understand how anyone could get by with so little.

These high salaries represent a breakthrough for GP's. For the first time, they're now earning more than the actors on *Casualty*.

There's a debate centering around unconventional medical practices within the NHS, such as keeping hospitals open and providing a bed straight away.

One of the controversial treatments under debate is the use of coffee enemas, in which a coffee solution is pumped into the body via the rectum.

Not only is its effectiveness in doubt, it'll probably get you thrown out of Starbucks.

One medical expert, Peter Fisher, told the *Guardian*: **'I don't know how homeopathy works.'**

Fair enough, except that he is: **'Peter Fisher, Director of the Royal Homeopathic Hospital.'**

'██████ SMILES WHEN YOU DRIVE WELL?'

PAUL MERTON: Oh, this is the happy goat. It's a new thing you can put on, now that the Christmas campaign's coming on for drink driving, you put a goat on the front of the bonnet of your car, and as long as it's connected up to your speedometer, and as long as you're within the correct speed – the goat smiles. And then if you go fast, it pulls a face. And it's easier for the police to spot, they just look, there's an unhappy goat, book him. And they drag you off and they read the goat's entrails and it tells you what speed you were doing. It's the happy goat that smiles when you drive well. Is that right? The new electric car from Japan.

DARA O'BRIAIN: Yes, the remarkable Toyota Pod £8,995, including road tax and goat.

'██████ TAKES HEAVY TOLL ON BEARS?'

PAUL MERTON: 'Loss of toilet facilities in woods.'

DARA O'BRIAIN: It's actually 'burger binge.' Bears in America are becoming obese after bingeing on left-overs they find when foraging in towns. According to one expert, **'In California, it's becoming increasingly common for residents to wake up and find an unwelcome, fat, furry visitor slumped in the kitchen.'** It's usually Kelly Osbourne, and it's a cry for help.

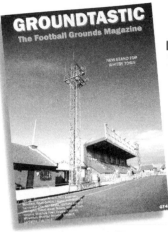

GROUNDTASTIC
The Football Grounds Magazine

NEW STAND FOR
WHITBY TOWN

DES LYNAM (GUEST HOST): Now here's that Missing Words round I promised you, featuring this week's guest publication: *Groundtastic*. I borrowed it from John Motson, in fact.

'WHY GO TO THE BEACH WHEN THERE'S ███████ TO VISIT?'

MARCUS BRIGSTOCKE: 'Elderly relatives with lots of cash'?

PAUL MERTON: 'A football league ground very near you'?

DES LYNAM: It's 'Bootham Crescent Stadium.'

PAUL MERTON: Which league are Bootham Crescent in at the moment?

DES LYNAM: They were relegated from Division Three. York City. Thank God there was something I knew here. It's sad about York this season, Ian, isn't it?

IAN HISLOP: Terrible.

DES LYNAM: Hmm. Why do you think that is?

IAN HISLOP: Did they lose to Lancaster?

ALEXANDER ARMSTRONG (GUEST HOST): Missing Words round is next. This week's guest publication is *Eurofruit*. Quite good for the first few issues, but then it all went a bit pear-shaped.

'WHO WANTS TO SMELL LIKE ▮▮▮▮▮▮?'

PAUL MERTON: 'A courgette.'

ALEXANDER ARMSTRONG: Not a fruit this time.

PAUL MERTON: A courgette's a vegetable.

HUGH FEARNLEY-WHITTINGSTALL: Actually, technically it's a fruit, because it's got the seeds on the inside and the fleshy bit on the outside, so technically it's a fruit.

PAUL MERTON: But, so, the seeds are on the inside it means it's a fruit?

HUGH FEARNLEY-WHITTINGSTALL: Oh it does, yeah.

PAUL MERTON: But what about a strawberry, it's got seeds on the outside. Why is that a fruit?

HUGH FEARNLEY-WHITTINGSTALL: Er, that is a ...

PAUL MERTON: You don't know, do you?

HUGH FEARNLEY-WHITTINGSTALL: That is a berry.

PAUL MERTON: It's a berry.

HUGH FEARNLEY-WHITTINGSTALL: It's a berry fruit.

PAUL MERTON: Oh, it's a berry fruit.

HUGH FEARNLEY-WHITTINGSTALL: It is a fruit, but it's an unusual fruit.

PAUL MERTON: Oh I suppose the clue's in the name.

HUGH FEARNLEY-WHITTINGSTALL: It's the only fruit with its seeds on the outside; it's the exception that proves the rule.

IAN HISLOP: Because you sounded a bit as though you were making it up.

HUGH FEARNLEY-WHITTINGSTALL: No. I stand by my fruity definitions.

PAUL MERTON: Yes he does. Is it, 'Who wants to smell like a budgie dipped in creosote?'

ALEXANDER ARMSTRONG: No, it's 'Sir Sniff Richard'. This is Sir Cliff launching his own range of perfumes.

IAN HISLOP: His new perfumes? What are they called?

ALEXANDER ARMSTRONG: There's to be an aftershave called 'Bachelor Boy'. Use it, and that's the way you'll stay.

'COR, ███████ IS A COOL NAME?'

PAUL MERTON: 'Apple'.

HUGH FEARNLEY-WHITTINGSTALL: That's Gwyneth Paltrow's new baby.

ALEXANDER ARMSTRONG (GUEST HOST): 'Apple' is the right answer, yeah. This is Chris Martin and Gwyneth Paltrow's baby, which they decided to call Apple. Gwyneth Paltrow told the *Express*, 'Apple is a very cool name'. Yes, it is, Gwyneth – for a fruit.

IAN HISLOP: But there are lots of people called fruits now, aren't there?

PAUL MERTON: Yeah.

IAN HISLOP: Peaches.

ALEXANDER ARMSTRONG: Cherie.

IAN HISLOP: Pomegranate Prescott.

ALEXANDER ARSTRONG: Yes, this is Gweneth Paltrow's new baby, Apple. According to the *Express*, **'It was a long and painful birth.'** In fact, they nearly called her Watermelon.

NEIL KINNOCK (GUEST HOST): As always, we conclude on the Missing Words round. This week's guest publication is *Windsock International* magazine. With this wonderful headline: **'Lights! Camera! Action! Fokkers!'**

'LONG TIME READERS OF *WINDSOCK* WILL ALREADY BE FAMILIAR WITH ███████ ███████ ███████ ?'

WILL SELF: 'Flatulence. Loneliness. Depression. Isolation.'

PAUL MERTON: 'Yawning chasms of boredom.'

WILL SELF: And psychosis.

IAN HISLOP: 'Loss of the will to live.'

LINDA SMITH: '*Windsock* readers' wives.'

NEIL KINNOCK: The actual answer is Leon Gimple's Photographs.

PAUL MERTON: How on earth are we meant to get that?!

NEIL KINNOCK: Well, I thought you'd be an avid reader of *Windsock* magazine.

PAUL MERTON: No, I went right off *Windsock* magazine years ago, no good any more.

IAN HISLOP: When it merged with *Windbag Weekly*.

PAUL MERTON: If I read anything about it now, I just read *Fokkers' Fortnightly*.

WILL SELF: That's like the low-budget one that grabbed all of *Windsock*'s readership, isn't it?

PAUL MERTON: That's right, yeah.

WILL SELF: Yeah, it was really sad that.

PAUL MERTON: With the centre page spread.

LINDA SMITH: Or the one that has royal approval, *Fokker's Three Weekly*.

O

ODD ONES OUT

JACK DEE (GUEST HOST): Which is the Odd One Out?

GEORGE W. BUSH   JONATHAN KING

DAVID BLAINE   THE CABINET

CLEMENT FREUD: Well, three of them are illusionists and one of them is just a paedophile.

IAN HISLOP: Is David Blaine still alive, as we speak?

JACK DEE: Who cares? But he is the odd one out because he's the only one who hasn't had his food tested.

PAUL MERTON: But how does the food testing work for Jonathan King? Does another prisoner sort of eat his dinner and say, 'Lovely, there was nothing wrong with that'?

JACK DEE: What did Tony Blair present George Bush with as a present earlier this year? Apart from the British Armed Forces?

CLEMENT FREUD: A Dunkin' Donut?

JACK DEE: It was actually a toilet bag.

CLEMENT FREUD: What's the difference?

JACK DEE: I don't know, because I've never tasted a Dunkin' Donut. Which implies I've eaten a toilet bag.

PAUL MERTON: We all get lonely.

JACK DEE: The answer is they have all had their food inspected before eating, apart from David Blaine, who has had his urine inspected by the *News of the World*.

In Bournemouth, Tony Blair's meals were checked because it was especially important during conference week that not even the food disagreed with him.

When David Blaine came out after 44 days in a box in central London, he was disorientated and confused. Although the biggest shock came when he got to the pay barrier at the NCP car park.

JOHN HUMPHRYS (GUEST HOST): Which is the Odd One Out?

BRITNEY SPEARS

EX-BBC CHAIRMAN, GAVYN DAVIES

MR AND MRS ALLOTT OF CONISBROUGH   THE RMT

IAN HISLOP: I think it's about houses. Because the RMT is the Rail Maritime and Transport Union, which are trying to kick John Prescott out of one of his homes. And Gavyn Davies has probably got a lot of homes, he's a multi-millionaire, and Britney Spears is buying a home in London.

PAUL MERTON: Mr and Mrs Allott don't have a home in London because they bought a house in Crystal Palace on the side of a hill and it was on wheels and it went all the way down and it's now in Middlesex, so it's not in London. So they're the odd one out, because their house travelled five hundred miles.

JOHN HUMPHRYS: Well, they are the odd one out. But the difference is, they chose to leave their home. And the reason why they chose to leave their home, do we know?

PAUL MERTON: Badgers impersonating them have convinced the local council that they were in fact the rightful owners.

JOHN HUMPHRYS: No, they chose to leave their home because it is in Butt Hole Road.

SEAN LOCK: Is that a cul-de-sac?

JOHN HUMPHRYS: What plans do the RMT have for John Prescott?

PAUL MERTON: They're going to turn him into a theme park. They're going to take all his innards out and put in rides for the little kiddies. Have you not heard about it, John? Next time you interview him, ask him. Ask him. Ask him where he keeps the ghost train. Underprivileged kids from the north east come down to London just to ride inside the Deputy Prime Minister.

JOHN HUMPHRYS: They've all taken legal action to evict someone, apart from Mr and Mrs Allott of Conisbrough, who moved out of their home in Butt Hole Road in South Yorkshire because they got sick of people joking about it.
John Prescott's affair with his secretary came as a surprise to his colleagues. According to the Mirror: **'The two of them were caught together in a lift.'** Presumably when the 'excess load' alarm went off.

ALEXANDER ARMSTRONG (GUEST HOST): Which is the Odd One Out?

BORIS BECKER   ARNOLD SCHWARZENEGGER

BRIGID O'SHAUGHNESSY   THE ZETA JONES DOUGLASES

PAUL MERTON: Brigid O'Shaughnessy is a fictional character. That's a still from *The Maltese Falcon.*

ALEXANDER ARMSTRONG: It's to do with something she does in the film. Something Ian knows everything about.

PAUL MERTON: Goats? Ah! She's a private investigator.

IAN HISLOP: Oh, I see, and I'm something to do with *Private Eye.* That's awfully good!

ALEXANDER ARMSTRONG: I know. I thought you'd like that.

PAUL MERTON: She's not a private investigator in the film – she hires one.

ALEXANDER ARMSTRONG: They have all hired a private detective to investigate someone else, except Arnold Schwarzenegger, who's hired someone to investigate his own groping past.

Talking about her early relationship with Michael Douglas, Catherine told reporters, **'When I first met Michael, I didn't want to jump straight into his bed.'** At least not while the safety bars and the IV drip were still there.

During Catherine's wedding to Michael Douglas, a member of the paparazzi sneaked into the reception.

According to the *Daily Mail,* **'He took a series of pictures with a secret camera hanging from the waistband of his trousers.'** He thought he had some great close-ups of Michael before realizing the camera was the wrong way round.

OFFENSIVE MATERIAL

If you are offended by any programme on the BBC, because of the content, the language or the general poor quality, you can telephone the 'Duty Log' and the 'Duty Officer' will write down your rantings and pass them on to any producers who can be arsed to read them. Try it, it's great fun (although don't ring when Graham Norton is on as the lines are usually quite busy).

Have I Got News For You receives several calls every week (curiously, there is always one from an 'unidentified' man who asks when Angus Deayton is coming back). The highest numbers of complaints come from specific groups of people who feel offended by jokes directly aimed at them. They are listed below.

We would like to find out how offensive these jokes really are, so to help us, you could try and embed yourself in a group of, say, Liverpudlians, read the relevant joke out loud and record the reaction. Send any interesting results to us at the usual address.

Women
Many feminists have applauded Margaret Beckett's appointment as the first-ever female Foreign Secretary, feeling that she'd be ideal to send to Iran, as she'd bring a feminine perspective to a major world problem. And a burkha wouldn't hurt, either.

Norfolk
A DNA testing company called Oxford Ancestors charges £195 to cover the costs involved in tracing your family roots. Although if you're from Norfolk, they'll do it for a fiver.

The Disabled
This is the story of a pensioner who was attacked by a Rottweiler and fought it off by hitting it with her false leg. When the story of the plucky one-legged woman appeared in the papers she received sympathetic phone calls, cards from well-wishers and the offer of a hot date from Paul McCartney.

Motherwell
A small amount of cannabis was found in John Reid's Lanarkshire home near Motherwell. It had a value of 85p, and that's after the housing boom.

Liverpool
After an article criticizing Liverpool's 'victim culture', *Spectator* editor Boris Johnson was forced to visit the city to apologise. It was appropriate that Boris went to Liverpool because, like everyone else there, he's got six jobs. The only difference is, Boris isn't claiming benefit as well.

Liverpudlians are of course very quick to take offence. And anything else they can lay their hands on.

Isle of Wight
In order to find out the difference in happiness levels between the present day and the 1950's, BBC researchers interviewed a sample of people living in England in 2006 and a sample of people living in the Isle of Wight in 2006.

Northerners
According to a recent report on child development: **'By the age of five, children should be developing climbing skills.'**

Or as they call it in Newcastle, burglary.

Women (again)
Reports are coming in of an outbreak of bird flu, or to give it its full Latin name, 'Panicus Tabloidus'.
Scientists say that the virus is destroyed by long exposure to heat, so the way British women cook turkey, we're safe. And it's unlikely that Brussels sprout fever will strike either.

Ventriloquists
Keith Harris's little friend Orville has been put down already. Nothing to do with bird flu, he's just an annoying green bastard.

P

PARADE

Often after a particularly convincing victory, Paul Merton will remind everyone that he has won not only many, many shows, but also many, many series.

Paul believes that there should be some official recognition of this achievement, especially as he only got CSE Metalwork and never reads the papers. He doesn't want much, just a small parade of 27 children with huge papier mâché heads fashioned in his own image, marching around the studio with placards declaring the score.

No-one on the show was sure quite how serious he was, until we found this drawing in his dressing room ...

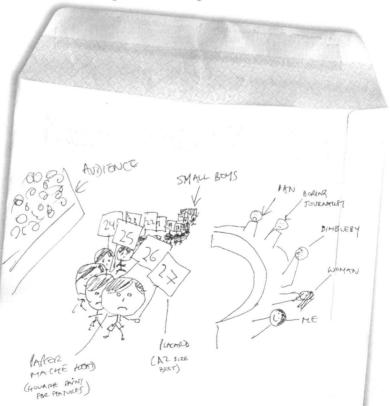

POT NOODLE

When Jack Dee hosted the show in June 2006, a new advertisement for a well-known noodles-in-a-plastic-cup snack had just appeared which featured Welsh miners digging noodles out of the ground ...

JACK DEE: Welsh people have said that a new Pot Noodle advert unfairly stereotypes them. Talking of Pot Noodles, a little bonus thing, does anyone know what they're calling the new vegetarian version in Korea?

IAN HISLOP: No?

JACK DEE: Not Poodles.

IAN HISLOP: Oh, that's terribly good.

PAUL MERTON: And for people who smoke cannabis, Pot Pot Noodles.

JOHN O'FARRELL: Cambodian dictator – Pol Pot Noodles.

PAUL MERTON: Is there a musical version coming out? 'Top of the Pot Noodles'?

JACK DEE: I so wish I could come up with one.

IAN HISLOP: For cranberry lovers, Piss Pot Noodles.

JACK DEE: There's one for babies, Cot Noodles ... Oh fuck off the lot of you.

PAUL MERTON: They've got one in Lancashire, have you heard about that? Hot Pot Noodles.

JACK DEE: There's one that you eat down caves, Pot ...

PAUL MERTON: Pot Hole Noodles?

JACK DEE: Thank you. At least let me get it out!

PAUL MERTON: I was trying to spread the blame around. This has been the best bit of the show! Forget all this 'who did this, he did that'. Make up names of Pot Noodles for half an hour, everybody's happy.

IAN HISLOP: There's one which the Met Police eat in their car: Shot Noodles.

LIZA TARBUCK: When you've got a cold, Snot Noodles.

JACK DEE: That's pretty much what they are if you haven't got a cold.

PAUL MERTON: They're doing a new version based on I Can't Believe It's Not Butter. Fuck me, it's Pot Noodles!

JACK DEE: New *Eastenders* one, Dot Noodles. I'm thinking, I'm thinking all the time, never stop.

PAUL MERTON: Have you been going through the alphabet – A, Bot, Dot, Fot ...

JOHN O'FARRELL: All this time and he got to D.

PAUL MERTON: D. Trying to work out 'Bot, Bosch, Bottom. Bottom Noodles.'

JACK DEE: There's more to come, there has to be.

PAUL MERTON: Ah, there's the one that's anonymous.

JACK DEE: What?

PAUL MERTON: What Noodles?

LIZA TARBUCK: Stop it.

JACK DEE: Yes, thank you for that ... There's the one you have on a boat, Yacht Noodles.

PAUL MERTON: You've gone to the other end of the alphabet now.

JOHN O'FARRELL: He thought, I'll start from the back, they won't notice. Spent 20 minutes going 'Zot Noodles?' It doesn't work!

JACK DEE: I didn't. The sad thing is, I went all the way through from the beginning and couldn't think of one until I got to Y.

After this show was broadcast, the makers of the famously hideous student snack were so chuffed with the free prime-time BBC1 publicity that they had to say thank you in the most lavish terms, and within days not one, but two trays of the stuff were delivered to the Have I Got News For You *production office in London – in two different flavours, ('Salty' and 'MSG').*

So, if you can think of any other words that sound like 'Pot', you could always add them to the word 'Noodle' and send them to: Unilever PLC, Unilever House, Blackfriars, London EC4P 4BQ
See if they send you anything back...

PROTOCOL

At a royal banquet, Prince Philip decides to entertain guests with a speech about his recent trip to China.

QUITE A FEW MORE ODD ONES OUT

KIRSTY YOUNG (GUEST HOST): Which is the Odd One Out?

MARGARET HODGE   JEFFREY ARCHER

NEIL HAMILTON   JONATHAN AITKEN

IAN HISLOP: I would guess this is a question about fighting libel actions. Margaret Hodge, I believe, is the odd one out, because she didn't actually fight the action. Jeffrey Archer said he would give up his job as Vice Chairman of the Tory Party, rather amusingly, to fight a libel action. Then Neil Hamilton was a backbencher, who asked questions for money, so he had to give that up for a bit.

JONATHAN AITKEN: Yes

IAN HISLOP: And Jonathan Aitken, who rather famously did that rather embarrassing number about the simple sword of truth and how you were going to stamp out the bent and twisted cancer of British journalism. I mean, I didn't take it personally. Though I have brought this with me ...

Ian gets out letter

It's about your bankruptcy, and *Private Eye* was one of your principal creditors, because we called you a liar. You probably remember. And you sued us, and then amusingly you went to jail for purgery. Um. Actually, I don't want to rake all this stuff up, it's ...

JONATHAN AITKEN: Go on.

IAN HISLOP: It's just that you owed us £28,000 in, you know, legal costs, obviously. We'd wasted all that money trying to prove something that was true. And we only got back 50 pence in the pound. I mean, I don't want to make a big deal of it, but it's £13,702 you owe me.

JONATHAN AITKEN: Yes. Sorry about that.

KIRSTY YOUNG: Anyone know what the Hamiltons have been up to lately? They've been advertising a CD called *Cheese Party*.

PAUL MERTON: Cheese party? Is this a whole phenomenon I've completely missed?

WILL SELF: Yeah, it's a party where a lot of people go round to each other's houses and get completely off their trolleys, sniffing cheese, eating it, all sorts of behaviour like that, spreading it on each other's bodies. Have you never been to one?

PAUL MERTON: No. I want to go. Will they be there?

WILL SELF: We've often thought of asking you, but you're just a bit straight, you know.

PAUL MERTON: Listen, give me a little slab of Edam and I'll show you another side of me.

KIRSTY YOUNG: Back to the question, please. They have all resigned from their jobs in order to fight a libel action, with the exception of Margaret Hodge. Jeffrey Archer is planning to run in next year's London Marathon, where he hopes to raise a record amount of money. And no doubt he will, providing he turns it into a sponsored kicking.

KIRSTY YOUNG (GUEST HOST): Which is the Odd One Out?

THE QUEEN MOTHER   JAMIE OLIVER

RICHARD DESMOND   BINGO FROM THE
                   BANANA SPLITS

PAUL MERTON: Is Bingo the only one that's come third in a Janet Street-Porter look-alike competition?

IAN HISLOP: Only one of them's a pornographer.

KIRSTY YOUNG: Is not the answer.

IAN HISLOP: It's true though.

WILL SELF: Only the Queen Mother has not received an honour.

IAN HISLOP: What did Bingo get?

WILL SELF: Bingo is Knight Commander of the British Empire.

KIRSTY YOUNG: There's a bit of a clue in the Jamie Oliver photograph. What's he holding?

PAUL MERTON: Drumsticks. Oh, Bingo was a drummer and Richard Desmond was a drummer. The Queen Mother was never a drummer, so she's the odd one out.

KIRSTY YOUNG: Well, yes. The Queen Mother couldn't play a full kit, but was apparently an expert on the bongos.

WILL SELF: You're making it up.

PAUL MERTON: If the Queen Mother played the bongos, we would have heard about it by now.

KIRSTY YOUNG: It's true. What other instrument could the Queen Mother play? Do you know?

IAN HISLOP: Spoons.

KIRSTY YOUNG: It's the harmonica. Her mother taught her to play the harmonica.

PAUL MERTON: That wonderful combination that you don't often hear enough, harmonica and bongos.

KIRSTY YOUNG: Yes. They are all drummers except the Queen Mother. According to the *Guardian*, **'Richard Desmond is an unorthodox businessman, who often takes duck hooters into meetings.'** Duck hooters, incidentally, are decoy whistles used by hunters and not the title of his latest magazine.

DARA O'BRIAIN (GUEST HOST): Which is the Odd One Out?

THE SAATCHI BROTHERS   GEORGE BUSH

SINBAD   GEORGE GALLOWAY

JOHN O'FARRELL: That's a very early photo of George Bush, isn't it.

IAN HISLOP: Or is that a child who's been called George Bush? This is an Iraqi question, because the Saatchi brothers were born in Baghdad. Sinbad was an Iraqi. This child, George Bush, was obviously born in Iraq. George Galloway wasn't born there, but would like to have been.

DARA O'BRIAIN: George, you weren't born in Baghdad, but you have visited there, how often?

GEORGE GALLOWAY: Oh, quite a few times.

JOHN O'FARRELL: And all those times that you've been to Hussein's and you've never had them back. Well Saddam and Mrs Hussein are probably sitting up in bed at this moment saying, 'You know, the Galloways never had us back, did they?'

DARA O'BRIAIN: George Galloway has met Saddam Hussein on a number of occasions, but, according to an old friend of his, **'The only living person Galloway's scared of is his wife.'** And she hasn't gassed any Kurds.

BORIS JOHNSON (GUEST HOST): Which is the Odd One Out?

SILVIO BERLUSCONI   THE QUEEN

MICHAEL HOWARD   THE MRSA SUPERBUG

PAUL MERTON: MRSA superbug, that's the bug that's in the hospitals at the moment, isn't it.

KATE GARRAWAY: Yeah. The one that's resilient to all sorts of anti-biotics. The Queen might have a stomach bug there and she's putting a brave face on it. And didn't Silvio, I might be massively libelling him, but didn't he get accused of bugging someone's office at some point?

BORIS JOHNSON: That's actually a brilliant answer.

KATE GARRAWAY: Is it?

BORIS JOHNSON: It's not wholly accurate, but it's ... I'll give you a clue. It's to do with cooking. It's actually to do with garlic.

IAN HISLOP: Oh that's right, she says: no garlic in my food.

BORIS JOHNSON: Correct.

IAN HISLOP: Does Berlusconi hate garlic?

BORIS JOHNSON: And the MRSA superbug is deterred by garlic.

IAN HISLOP: Oh well, that's the first bit of useful information we've ever had on this programme.

BORIS JOHNSON: Er, er ... *(Boris is looking through the cards)*

PAUL MERTON: Have you lost something, Boris?

IAN HISLOP: What he's lost is some joke about Michael Howard, garlic and being one of the undead.

BORIS JOHNSON: Absolutely, er, not. Right ...

PAUL MERTON: Boris, I think you should have your own radio station. Boris FM, we've just tuned-in, just to try and listen to you construct a sentence.

BORIS JOHNSON: How did, how did John Reid, the Health Secretary, react to the discovery?

IAN HISLOP: He did what the government always does, he appointed an infection Tsar.

BORIS JOHNSON: As in a Tsar is Born. Now ...

PAUL MERTON: Or I Was Born Under A Squandering Tsar.

BORIS JOHNSON: Which is exactly what happens under this government, I mean they have a Tsar for everything, don't they?

PAUL MERTON: That's right.

BORIS JOHNSON: That's a very good slogan.

KATE GARRAWAY: You're going to use that, aren't you?

IAN HISLOP: The Tory Party is alive!

PAUL MERTON: And reeking of garlic.

BORIS JOHNSON: Anyway, Silvio Berlusconi says he associates garlic with: **'boredom and death.'** So they get Delia Smith in Italy, too. I think that's a bit unfair on old Delia, isn't it?

RICK WAKEMAN: Yes.

BORIS JOHNSON: Claiming he'd been misquoted in a recent interview, Silvio Berlusconi said, **'It was the end of a very long day. We had a bottle of champagne ... Boris Johnson took advantage of me.'** Well, there you go, that's ... You know how it is. It was a long, it was actually, it was a torrid evening in, as you can imagine ...

REALIZATION

In a Westminster pub, one customer is suddenly dismayed to discover that his wallet isn't in his other suit.

RING TONES

The show has always moved with the times.
Download these now!

TOP 16 RING TONES

Angus Deayton	'ALLEGEDLY'	12121	12221
Paul Merton	'IS IT LULU?'	34343	34443
Ian Hislop	'DON'T Y'KNOW?'	56565	56665
Paul Merton	'METALWORK CSE – UNGRADED'	78787	78887
Boris Johnson	'CRIPES!'	90909	90009
Bruce Forsyth	'... NEWS, FOR YOU, HAVE I GOT!'	10101	10001
Angus Deayton	'IN WHAT WAY?'	23232	32323
Ian Hislop	'THE LAWYERS ARE WATCHING'	45454	54545
Paul Merton	'WHERE'S MY PARADE?'	67676	76767
Alexander Armstrong	'AT THE END OF ROUND ONE, THE SCORES ARE FOUR-ALL'	01012	01013
Dara O'Briain	'AT THE END OF ROUND ONE, THE SCORES ARE FOUR-ALL'	01014	01015
John Humphrys	'AT THE END OF ROUND ONE, THE SCORES ARE FOUR-ALL'	01016	01017
Lorraine Kelly	'AT THE END OF ROUND ONE, THE SCORES ARE FOUR-ALL'	01018	01019
John Sergeant	'AT THE END OF ROUND ONE, THE SCORES ARE FOUR-ALL'	01020	01021
Kirsty Young	'AT THE END OF ROUND ONE, THE SCORES ARE FOUR-ALL'	01022	01023
Various	'THIS WEEK'S WINNER IS PAUL'	89898	98989

S

SAUSAGES

PAUL MERTON: Man who didn't become Pope is inconsolable.

JO CAULFIELD: Man from Newcastle on night out.

PAUL MERTON: Frozen sausage killer, suspect arrested.

SCANDAL

A cheese slice at Greggs the Bakers NOW COSTS £1.25

SCORES

If you ask people whether the scores on *Have I Got News For You* matter or not, the responses vary considerably – Paul says they do matter, Ian insists strongly that they don't. One thing everyone agrees on, however, is that none of the participants has the slightest clue as to how the points are awarded to begin with. Here, for the first time, we can reveal the basic rules by which the points are allocated.

SCORING SYSTEM

In **Round One**, points are awarded for the accuracy and wittiness of the answer – in other words, the accuracy. Additional points may be scored by the opposing team on any given question if a) the team whose question it is hasn't been funny yet, and b) the opposing team includes someone the host really fancies. Further points can be won in a number of ways:

> **i)** by a successful challenge as to the veracity of an opponent's answer
>
> **ii)** by gambling to double the value of points won so far, in a gambit indicated by taking a sip of water before answering, but ONLY on the opposing team's question
>
> **iii)** by cheating.

At the end of Round One, despite all these variables, the host must silently declare 'quits' and the points are 'rounded down' to two each.

Round Two is scored in the same way as Round One, with the exception that the audience's favourite ploy, the 'counter-pass cross-play' now comes into effect – but, obviously, only on alternate questions. An extra point may be awarded if either Ian or Paul correctly guesses the host's secret 'Word of the Week', and then includes three synonyms for it in their final answer, without their team-mate realizing. Where appropriate, over-bidding is now allowed, following the 2005 Pontefract Amendment.

The **Odd One Out round** is scored thus: a point is awarded if the solution to formula below is greater than, or equal to, 1:

$$\frac{a}{b} \times \frac{2c + dr^2}{e} \div \frac{a}{c}$$

where a = Ian's post-rant blood pressure
b = Ian's guest's age (to nearest 100 if Bill Deedes)
c = the albedo, or reflective index, of Paul's shirt this week
d = Paul's guest's cholesterol count
e = how funny the picture of Margaret Beckett is.

In the final **Missing Words round**, points are awarded according to who's read the most newspapers that week.

STOP PRESS

It may surprise viewers to learn that one of the drawbacks of working in topical comedy and contemporary satire is that you're having to make up jokes about the bloody news all the time. Talk about dull! And another major pain is that, frequently, these jokes can then be overtaken by events, thus rendering them rather less funny than they were, originally. (If they ever were funny – or, indeed, original.)

To ensure that this particular book isn't entirely out of date by the time you read it – because we actually had to write it months ago – here's a special section for you to complete for yourself, thereby guaranteeing that one bit, at least, will possess a vague semblance of topicality. Simply fill in the blanks and create your own up-to-the-minute news round-up.

UK POLITICS

The _____ Government of Prime Minster _____ _____ ended 200_ reeling from a series of increasingly squalid scandals involving leading members of the Cabinet. First, there was the lurid expose of the _____ Secretary's irregular _____ practices, so far never fully explained, despite the belated and bungled attempt to pin the blame on the _____, and the subsequent findings of the _____ Report, which completely cleared the Minister of any wrongdoing. Then a disbelieving nation was presented with the now-infamous

CCTV footage of the Minister for _____ , openly _____ing
in public with a _____ _____ ____—____ _____,
which led to a messy resignation and the possibility of
criminal proceedings. Then came the most potentially
damaging revelation of all. A tabloid journalist, disguised as
a _____ _____, managed to deceive the Minister for
_____ into revealing what are claimed to be secret
Government proposals to introduce compulsory _____
for all _____. A spokesman for the Minister denied the
allegations, saying, 'This is utter nonsense. There are
absolutely no plans to _____ any _____, or even to _____
them, no matter how great the financial benefits.'

Prime Minister _____ _____ is himself under fire, following
claims that his wife, _____, is alleged to have _____
_____ a _____ in the Far East, without revealing that
she'd previously been _____ _____.

Meanwhile, the Opposition leader, _____ _____, is
attempting to raise morale in his own party, following the
shock disclosure that, contrary to his earlier claims, he never
actually _____ his _____, but had merely _____
_____ _____ instead, before _____ _____ _____
in an attempt to conceal the truth from his colleagues.

SPORT

This year proved another _____ly poor year for British sport.
The Wembley fiasco drags on, with the completion date now
estimated at 201_. In football, there were regular ugly scenes of
mass brawling between the players of _____ and Manchester
United. Premiership fans continue to desert the game,
claiming that Chelsea have killed off any vestige of excitement,
having spent £_,250 million on new players. Wayne Rooney
continues to grab the headlines after _____ _____ _____
with fiancée Coleen, in a Liverpool _____. And spare a
thought for Michael Owen, whose latest _____ injury sees
him sidelined for another ___ months.

In cricket, England's hopes of a return to form, following the
hard-fought draw in the series against a lowly _____ _____ side,
were crushed after being whitewashed by a much-weakened
_____ team. Freddie Flintoff's antics on tour, when he _____
his _____ with a _____ didn't help matters much, either – and
saying he was _____ isn't really an excuse.

The less said about tennis, the better. Once again, British
interest at a rainy Wimbledon promptly ceased after the
second round. A dull predictable Men's Final, won by top
seed _____ _____ over outsider _____ _____, was
enlivened only when a _____ briefly interrupted play, much
to the crowd's amusement.

MEDIA AND ARTS

This year's Turner Prize whipped up the usual storm of
controversy. The work of the winner, a _____ian sculptor
from _____, raised many eyebrows through its inventive
use of materials such as _____, _____, raw sewage, _____,
blood and _____ – though many felt the prize should have
gone to the video installations of the _____ish film-
maker from _____, with their depiction of ____ _____,
rotting _____, slow-motion _____ _____, and a man in
a room constantly _____ his _____ while blind-folded.

On TV, ratings-topper *I'm A Celebrity* ... saw the unlikely jungle
victory of _____ _____, despite having accidentally
swallowed _____ _____ _____early in the series.

Meanwhile, the BBC announced its plans to _____ _____
_____ ____ _____ ___ _____ _____. A BBC spokeswoman
said, 'Times change, and so must we. Which is why we're
launching a new series, all about _____ _____ _____,
to be hosted by _____ _____. It'll be absolutely _____.'

And Ben Elton's latest musical '_____ _____', based on
the works of _____ _____, with _____ _____ in the
lead role, opened in the West End to huge success, despite
being _____.

CELEBRITY AND TRIVIA

The year ended in heartbreak for Victoria Beckham, who lost ____ _____ ____ _____ _____ ____. Jonathan Ross finally _____ _____ his ____ to ____ ____ ____. Rebecca Loos gained further notoriety, after she ____ a _____ _____ in a _____ _____.

Darren Day sadly called off his engagement to _____ _____. Jade Goody confessed she didn't know how to _____ _____ _____ without _____. George Michael was found ____ing his ____ in a London _____.

Elton John flew into a rage live on TV, after being _____ ____ ____ _____ with the wrong ____. Madonna revealed that she and husband Guy Ritchie always _____ _____ ____ their _____ _____. Neil and Christine Hamilton agreed to _____ all their _____ ____ _____ and _____. Kate Moss was seen _____ing _____ behind _____ _____ _____. Michael Winner admitted he was _____ _____ ____ _____. And Chantelle _____ _____ _____ _____ despite _____ _____ _____. Oh, and *Big Brother* was, once again, an amoral pile of festering shite.

WORLD POLITICS

The international situation continued to deteriorate as the year wore on. President Bush, having ignored world opinion and invaded _____, ostensibly to bring about _____ _____ _____ but, in reality, with a view to _____ its _____ supplies, then turned his attention to the neighbouring state of _____. Warning them against further testing of their new _____ _____, the President claimed that they also had plans to increase the size of their _____ _____ _____, and that such a move threatened the stability of the region.

In France, further outbreaks of rioting were provoked by changes in the law concerning _____ _____ and _____, which saw thousands of _____ take to the streets, setting fire to _____ and _____ _____.

And a major diplomatic row was sparked off between Britain and _____, following remarks by Prince Philip about the _____ _____ of the local _____ _____.

With only slight amendments, this entire section can be re-used, year after year. Photocopy the pages, and give it a try.

STUDIO SET

A state-of-the-art set, crafted by a leading designer, can impart a strong 'brand identity' to a TV programme, creating a striking ambience and achieving a compelling visual effect. We got ours by hacking up the old *Blankety Blank* set and giving it a lick of paint. Here are just a few of its unique features ...

KEY

1 Host's seat
2 Ian's seat
3 Paul's seat
4 Jug of water
5 Mug of Ovaltine
6 Tin of creosote
7–9 Cameras for filming programme
10 Camera for filming back of bald men's heads in audience during end-credits
11 Desk screen to show clips and stills
12 Desk screen to show clips, stills and DVDs of Chaplin, Keaton, Laurel and Hardy
13–18 Executive Producer's lottery numbers
19 Entrances to teams' escape tunnel (Neil Kinnock episode)
20–1 Odds against Ian winning
22 Audience members (good-looking)
23 Audience members (shockers)
24 Audience members (rowdy, fans of Ian)
25 Audience members (rowdy, fans of Paul)
26 Prompter, under desk, with cattle-prod
27 Large IKEA rug, covering stain on floor where Charles Kennedy was sick
28 Backdrop
29 Backdrop with subliminal message 'Why not buy several copies of the *HIGNFY* book? It's reasonably priced and makes an excellent gift for any occasion.'
30 Backdrop with arrow drawn on it in pencil by Paul, so it looks like it's sticking through head of Ian's guests
31 (88°F) sunny, very hot
32 Position of backdrop turner
33 Position of ambidextrous backdrop turner
34 Mad woman with cackling laugh, who always sits directly beneath microphone
35 Site of cursed Stone Age pagan burial mound, bringing doom and defeat to all who dare disturb it
36 Forty-piece live band for theme tune
37 Autocue machine

38 Autocue machine (Ronnie Corbett episode)
39 Boris Johnson, still lost from last programme
40 Red disc numbered '40', lying on floor, no-one knows why
41 Five-foot long trench cut into floor, for presenter's legs (Jeremy Clarkson, Dara O'Briain episodes)
42 Book depository
43 Presidential car
44 Position of second gunman
45 Geoff Hurst
46 Ball
47 Russian linesman

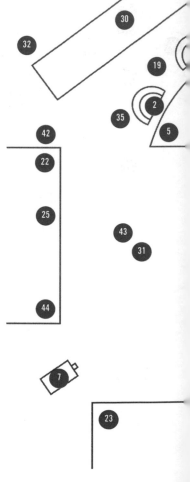

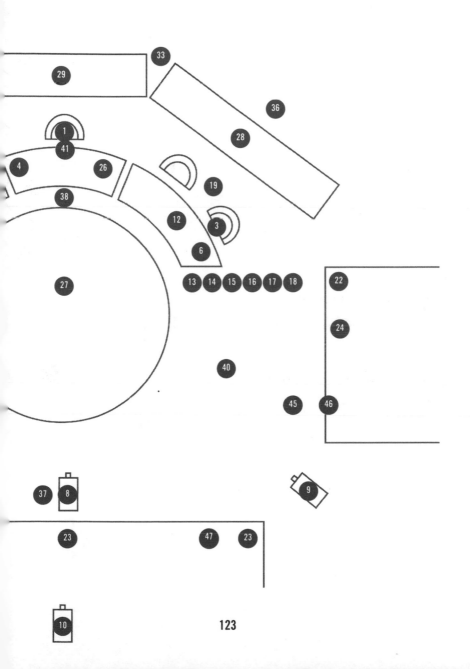

SUDOKU

The harsher critics of *Have I Got News For You* are quick to point out that, far from being refreshingly satirical, the show just trots out the same basic, broadly offensive autocue gags, over and over again. Well spotted, them.

So how do the writers give the appearance of variety when, in fact, no more than nine such pithy barbs are ever used? They cleverly employ an ancient Japanese method, which many national newspapers have recently used to boost their circulation.

You too can see what it is like to put together a topical comedy show script by playing *Have I Got News For You* Sudoku. Each comedically-honed observation must appear only once in each row, column and 3 x 3 box. Have fun!

RATING: SIMPLE
Solution on page 157

		MENZIES IS OLD	CAMILLA ISN'T PRETTY		BLAIR TELLS LIES			CAMERON IS POSH
	CAMERON IS POSH				KILROY-SILK IS ORANGE			BLAIR TELLS LIES
			BROWN IS MISERLY				MENZIES IS OLD	CAMILLA ISN'T PRETTY
		NORFOLK IS BACKWARD			PRESCOTT IS FAT		BUSH IS STUPID	
	KILROY-SILK IS ORANGE						CAMILLA ISN'T PRETTY	
	BLAIR TELLS LIES		CAMERON IS POSH			NORFOLK IS BACKWARD		
BLAIR TELLS LIES	BROWN IS MISERLY				NORFOLK IS BACKWARD			
NORFOLK IS BACKWARD			PRESCOTT IS FAT				BROWN IS MISERLY	
CAMILLA ISN'T PRETTY			BUSH IS STUPID		BROWN IS MISERLY	KILROY-SILK IS ORANGE		

TELL-TALE SIGNS

Britain's least-convincing transvestite admits the hands are usually the giveaway.

THIS IS WHERE WE HAVE PUT SOME MORE ODD ONES OUT

GREG DYKE (GUEST HOST): Which is the Odd One Out?

JOHN MAJOR   ALASTAIR CAMPBELL

WILLIAM THE CONQUEROR   A PEAR

IAN HISLOP: It's to do with bastards, isn't it?

GREG DYKE: Explain a bit more.

IAN HISLOP: Well, John Major famously said off-air that a number of members of his Cabinet were bastards. William the Conqueror, was he the bastard son?

GREG DYKE: Yeah.

IAN HISLOP: And most pears are bastards.

ARMANDO IANNUCCI: Bastards, yes.

IAN HISLOP: Because you buy them and you think they're going to ripen and they never do, and they're really hard.

PAUL MERTON: Campbell's the odd one out.

GREG DYKE: Why?

PAUL MERTON: Because you called him a bastard.

GREG DYKE: The answer is they've all been called bastards, apart from Alastair Campbell, who during the dodgy dossier inquiry was referred to as 'the C word'.

ARMANDO IANNUCCI: Someone threw eggs at him this week. Students are always throwing dairy products at British politicians. Flour and eggs, but why don't they all come together and just throw a big cake?

GREG DYKE: And who else do we know who was caught out by a microphone that he thought wasn't turned on?

DANNY BAKER: Ron Atkinson, of course. But if anyone's ever listened to Ron Atkinson commentating over the last 15 years, I always presumed he didn't know the mic was on anyway.

GREG DYKE: Of course, and the pear is the Bloody Bastard pear.

PAUL MERTON: Is it?

GREG DYKE: Yes. There's also a plum, you know, called the 'Shit Smock.'

PAUL MERTON: Shit Smock plum? I wouldn't send Ron Atkinson to get them, I tell you.

GREG DYKE: You got that right, they've all been called bastards, apart from Alastair Campbell, who during the dodgy dossier inquiry was referred to as 'the C word'. Not to mention 'the T word', 'the F word' and 'the W word'. And that was just in my office ...

DES LYNAM (GUEST HOST): What was Lawrence of Arabia's distinguishing feature?

T. E. LAWRENCE   KELVIN MACKENZIE

RICHARD DESMOND   WILSON, KEPPLE AND BETTY

PAUL MERTON: He was born in Carshalton.

DES LYNAM: He had scars on both buttocks. That's public school for you there, Ian.

PAUL MERTON: Are they in the shape of Z's? He might have been buggered by Zorro.

IAN HISLOP: No, Zorro was in the year below.

DES LYNAM: The answer is they've all impersonated Arabs, except for Richard Desmond, who this week caused offence by impersonating a Nazi.

Before his death in 1935, T. E. Lawrence considered how he might be remembered: **'In the distant future, if the distant future deigns to consider my insignificance, I shall be appraised rather as a man of letters than a man of action.'**
Sorry mate, TV quiz show, Odd One Out, dressed as an Arab.

TOFFS

PAUL MERTON: 'Technically, I should be in the race, but you know how it is, I got so bored, I thought what the hell.'

WILL SELF: Shergar and Lord Lucan have a drink at Royal Ascot.

PAUL MERTON: David Cameron puts on dark glasses as he has a flashback.

TONY BLAIR

An incriminating photo from Tony Blair's gap year sheds new light on his fondness for Europe.

Defending his latest initiative, Blair told the CBI: **'Every single difficult decision I have taken has resulted in predictions of disaster, shrieks of outrage, and determined resistance.'**

Well, there is one decision he could take that wouldn't get that reaction.

(Nice little joke there sent into us by Mr G. Brown.)

TOP TRUMPS

Since all that unpleasant business in 2002, the show has been presented by a number of guest hosts. Some have been great, while some have been Neil Kinnock. But which one is the best of the bunch? There's only one way to find out – and that's to play a game of Top Trumps. It's the fun way to see how your favourite presenter measures up!

HAVE I GOT NEWS FOR YOU

JEREMY CLARKSON

AGE: 46
HEIGHT: 6' 5" (he's fucking huge)
SHOWS HOSTED: 3
CATCHPHRASES: 1 – 'Unleash the beast!'
SPECIALITY: 25 – (grand per week from column)

HAVE I GOT NEWS FOR YOU

BORIS JOHNSON

AGE: 42 (mental age 6)
HEIGHT: 6' 0"
SHOWS HOSTED: 3
CATCHPHRASES: minus 2
SPECIALITY: 1,104 – (average no. lines fluffed per show)

HAVE I GOT NEWS FOR YOU

RONNIE CORBETT

AGE: 76
HEIGHT: 5' 1" (no he isn't)
SHOWS HOSTED: 1
CATCHPHRASES: 2 – 'My producer said to me ...'
'So it's goodnight from me ...'
SPECIALITY: 155 – (height in centimetres – sounds better!)

HAVE I GOT NEWS FO

BRUCE FORSYTH

AGE: 117
HEIGHT: 5' 11" (5' 10" without toupee)
SHOWS HOSTED: 1
CATCHPHRASES: 264 ...
4, 260, ...catch-phrases!
SPECIALITY: 115 – (years in showbiz)

CHARLOTTE CHURCH

AGE: 20
HEIGHT: 5' 2"
SHOWS HOSTED: 1
CATCHPHRASES: 1 – 'Same again, please.'
SPECIALITY: 134 – (pre-show fags)

ANGUS DEAYTON

AGE: 50
HEIGHT: 5' 9" (yes, TV can be deceptive)
SHOWS HOSTED: 198
CATCHPHRASES: 3 – 'Allegedly.'
'In what way?'
'It won't happen again, I promise.'
SPECIALITY: 198 – (free designer suits in wardrobe)

DARA O'BRIAIN

AGE: 35
HEIGHT: 6' 4"
SHOWS HOSTED: 4
CATCHPHRASES: 1 – 'Och, aye, the noo!' (check this – ed)
SPECIALITY: 602 – (words spoken per minute)

HAVE I GOT NEWS FOR YOU

DES LYNAM

AGE: 64
HEIGHT: 6' 1"
SHOWS HOSTED: 3
CATCHPHRASES: 1 – 'Hey, guys – tell you what ...'
SPECIALITY: 135 – (Kama Sutra positions mastered)

HAVE I GOT NEWS FOR YOU

KIRSTY YOUNG

AGE: 38
HEIGHT: 5' 7"
SHOWS HOSTED: 4
CATCHPHRASES: 1 – 'Your eighth and final record?'
SPECIALITY: 129 – (fantasy websites devoted to her)

HAVE I GOT NEWS FOR YOU

CAROL VORDERMAN

AGE: 46
HEIGHT: 5' 6"
SHOWS HOSTED: 1
CATCHPHRASES: 2 – 'Two off the top, and one off the bottom.'
'We offer a flexible, affordable loan with a single monthly repayment.'
SPECIALITY: 151 – (25 times the 4, 6 times the 8, plus the 2, plus the 1 = 151. But there's several ways you could do it.)

GOT NEWS FOR YOU

NEIL KINNOCK

AGE: 64
HEIGHT: 5' 9"
SHOWS HOSTED: 1
CATCHPHRASES: 1 – 'That might well indeed be the case, but I refer you, if I may, to an earlier instance, quoted by my esteemed colleague who, it must be said … etc. etc.'
SPECIALITY: 137 – (minutes' duration – longest speech without drawing breath)

HAVE I GOT NEWS FOR YOU

WILLIAM HAGUE

AGE: 45
HEIGHT: 5' 11"
SHOWS HOSTED: 3
CATCHPHRASES: 1 – 'Most of you won't be here in 30 or 40 years' time.'
SPECIALITY: 100 – (% light reflected off head)

HAVE I GOT NEWS F...

JOAN COLLINS

AGE: 39
HEIGHT: 5' 6"
SHOWS HOSTED: 1
CATCHPHRASES: 2 – 'Hello, young man ...'
'I'm 73, you know ... oops.'
SPECIALITY: 121 – (hours in make-up)

TREVOR McDONALD AS GUEST HOST

TREVOR McDONALD: This is the David Mills/Tessa Jowell/ Berlusconi saga. For all the details, over to you Ian.

IAN HISLOP: Oh, live. Thanks Trevor. Well, I don't know much about what's happening at the moment.

MARCUS BRIGSTOCKE: I'm sitting near Ian Hislop at the moment and I can confirm that nothing's happening. Paul.

PAUL MERTON: And can I just come in there?

MARCUS BRIGSTOCKE: Over to you.

PAUL MERTON: Can I just come in? I've just got Birmingham two, West Bromwich Albion one. Back to you Trevor.

TREVOR McDONALD: Thank you. David Mills did legal work for Mr Berlusconi. Remortgaged his house, paid off the mortgage in a few months.

PAUL MERTON: Sorry, but there's an equalizer there from West Bromwich Albion. Beautiful move there up the pitch. Klinsmann's back, Tony Blair in the far corner. Wonderful goal, wonderful goal. Back to you there, Trevor.

TREVOR McDONALD: Thank you. Mills admitted that originally ...

IAN HISLOP: Apparently there are going to be scattered showers.

TREVOR McDONALD: Thank you very much, Ian. Yes, this is the Italian elections. Silvio Berlusconi lost the elections by 0.1% of the vote. After hearing the news, George Bush immediately rang him up to congratulate him on his landslide victory.

'UNAVAILABILITY'

Some genuine correspondence ...

FROM THE EDITOR

BY FAX

TO: ███████
Have I Got News For You

FROM: Piers Morgan

DATE: 14th March 2001

Dear ███████

Thank you for your kind invitation.

I would rather staple my eyelids to Hislop's arse....

Kind regards

Piers Morgan

MGN Limited
One Canada Square Canary Wharf London E14 5AP
Switchboard: 0207 293 3000 / 0207 510 3000   Fax: 0207 293 3405 / 0207 510 3405   Telex: 27286   Cables: Mirror London E14
MGN Limited Registered Office: One Canada Square Canary Wharf London E14 5AP Registered No. 2571173 England and Wales
A Trinity Mirror business

'TO SAVE MONEY, USE AN OLD UMBRELLA AS ▬▬▬▬ ?'

PAUL MERTON: 'A salad spinner.'

P. J. O'ROURKE: 'Birth control device.'

ROBIN COOK (GUEST HOST): You're just boasting again P. J.

IAN HISLOP: 'An umbrella.' That would save money.

PAUL MERTON: Is it 'poncho'? It's written on the autocue just there, look.

ROBIN COOK: 'To save money, use an old umbrella as a poncho for a small child.' Sending your child out in an old umbrella will save you a lot of money, as they'll get taken into care and you won't have to pay for them any more.

'CAN'T AFFORD TO SEND YOUR LITTLE DARLINGS TO ETON? THEN ██████ ?'

PAUL MERTON: 'Shoot yourself, life's not worth living'.

ADAM HART DAVIS: 'Buy them the board game instead'.

JACK DEE (GUEST HOST): I think you're absolutely right there. Yes, 'buy them the board game instead', word for word. It's the Eton housemaster who's invented a board game based on life at the famous public school. He says if it's a success, he'll bring out a state school version, in which, if you throw three double sixes in a row, you still don't get anywhere.

'GIANT BUNNY SUFFERING FROM ██████ ?'

PAUL MERTON: 'Plankton poisoning'.

IAN HISLOP: 'Elephantisis'. Rare for a rabbit, but ...

ROSS NOBLE: 'Giant bunny suffering from claustrophobia inside tiny top hat'.

ANDREW MARR (GUEST HOST): The correct answer is in fact 'a broken heart'. This is Tinkerbell, the British Giant Rabbit, left devastated after her long-term mate died. According to the *Daily Express*, the British giant rabbit is: **'Sociable, thrives on interacting with people and has 10-inch ears.'** Sorry, that's my CV.

'HAVE THEY GOT ███████ FOR YOU?'

IAN HISLOP: 'Shoes'.

PAUL MERTON: 'Zoos'.

DES LYNAM (GUEST HOST): No.

PAUL MERTON: 'Loos'.

KAYE ADAMS: Loos?

PAUL MERTON: 'Cruise'.

IAN HISLOP: 'Booze'.

DES LYNAM: No, its 'Phews'.

IAN HISLOP: Phews?

DES LYNAM: Yes.

KAYE ADAMS: Oh, phews.

DES LYNAM: This is a study which has found that men watching female newsreaders tend to gawp at the presenter and don't listen to what's being said. Incidentally ladies, if you didn't catch any of that, don't worry, it wasn't important.

'LASAGNE IS THE NEW ▬▬▬▬?'

IAN HISLOP: 'Tagliatelle'.

DAVE GORMAN: 'Fish and chips'.

PAUL MERTON: 'Penicillin'.

JOHN BIRD: 'Buggery'.

KIRSTY YOUNG (GUEST HOST): 'Lasagne is the new Chicken Tikka Masala'.

One supermarket spokesman said, **'We've seen quite a lasagne surge in the High Street.'** Yeah, usually outside pubs at closing time.

'▬▬ IS A HIDEOUS WAY TO LOSE SHEEP?'

PAUL MERTON: 'Giving them a map that's false'. A backward map. Giving them spam, which is 'maps' backwards, is a hideous way to lose sheep. Blindfolding them and putting them in the back of a car and then letting them out and they don't know where they are. And then the police have to come and the sheep say, 'Well, I heard a church bell near a railway station', and then the police piece out where it was. I do actually know this. It's 'bloat'.

'YOU DRANK MY ▮▮▮▮ ?'

PAUL MERTON: 'Mother-in-law'?

IAN HISLOP: Is it 'Horlicks'?

MARCUS BRIGSTOCKE (GUEST HOST): You're not a million miles away with mother-in-law.

IAN HISLOP: Is it 'blood, Mr Howard'?

TONY LIVESEY: '... sister-in-law'.

PAUL MERTON: My 'sister-in-law's blood'. In a bizarre satanic ritual in Halifax.

MARCUS BRIGSTOCKE: It is, in fact, 'You drank my grandad'.

IAN HISLOP: Yeah, this is someone's ashes, isn't it? Being put into a cup of tea?

MARCUS BRIGSTOCKE: Yes. In the Czech Republic, some drunken friends accidentally drank their grandfather's ashes, mistaking them for instant coffee. They realized their mistake when they noticed that the coffee tasted of Werther's Originals.

URINE

PAUL MERTON: 'OK, now we've pissed in them, remember Kilroy Silk's just coming round the corner.'

V

VARIOUS MISSING WORDS

'ELF MEN JAILED FOR ███████ ?'

JULIA HARTLEY-BREWER: 'Holding bonsai tree-top protest'.

PAUL MERTON: 'Gnome abuse'.

PHILL JUPITUS: 'Hobbit fondling'.

PAUL MERTON: And 'orc squeezing'.

IAN HISLOP: No, it's corruption. It's the French petrol firm Elf.

ALEXANDER ARMSTRONG (GUEST HOST): You're absolutely right, Elf men ...

IAN HISLOP: And they bribed a lot of French politicians. I don't want to harp on about this European corruption theme, but have a look.

ALEXANDER ARMSTRONG: That's right, the answer is 'stealing 210 million pounds'. This, of course, refers to fraudulent oil company executives from France and not to the race of tiny, funny faced, half-human mischief-makers. But I can see why you'd be confused.

'IF YOU'RE ██████ WHEN YOU'RE OLD, THERE'S SOMETHING WRONG WITH YOU?'

PAUL MERTON: 'Seven'.

JULIA HARTLEY-BREWER: 'Dead'.

IAN HISLOP: Is it 'celibate'?

PAUL MERTON: Is it 'Sellafield'? Is it 'Sellotape'?

ALEXANDER ARMSTRONG (GUEST HOST): No.

PAUL MERTON: It could be one of them.

ALEXANDER ARMSTRONG: No, the answer is, 'If you're still acting'. That's Jane Horrocks, who claims that actors get madder and madder as they get older. Nonsense, just look at Brian Blessed.

'██████ STARTLES SPACEMEN?'

IAN HISLOP: 'Labour MP in his underpants'?

PAUL MERTON: 'David Bowie'.

DARA O'BRIAIN (GUEST HOST): 'Odd noise', is the correct answer. According to the *Guardian*, 'Two astronauts on the international space station were disturbed by a muffled bang coming from the area of the sleeping quarters and lavatory.' It was followed, apparently, by an alien emerging and saying, 'I'd give that a couple of your Earth minutes.'

WALLPAPERS

The show has always moved with the times. Download these now!

WALLPAPERS

10101

10102

10103

10104

10105

10106

10107

10108

10109

WILDLIFE

In the Lake District, soup of the day is prepared at the Beatrix Potter snack bar.

WORLD CUP FLOP

PAUL MERTON: This is Theo Walcott, who was a surprising picking for the England squad.

MICHAEL BUERK (GUEST HOST): Where did Sven spot him?

IAN HISLOP: He's never seen him play.

DAVID MITCHELL: He put 'football' into Google.

IAN HISLOP: I went out to dinner when the semi-final of the World Cup was on, when Germany won. Rather stupidly, I was in a German car, came down Shaftesbury Avenue to Leicester Square, surrounded by thugs: 'Look, it's a German car.'

Thumps desk

PAUL MERTON: It's very sweet of you to think they were attacking you because of the car Ian.

MICHAEL BUERK: Yes, this was the selection of Theo

Walcott, an untried teenager, for England's 2006 World Cup squad.

To make the journey to games comfortable, the England team's £400,000 tour bus was fitted with the latest state-of-the-art equipment. However, they still had to put up with Walcott sitting in the back of the coach saying, 'Are we there yet?'

WHERE ARE THEY NOW?

Television is well-known as a cosy, friendly, generous business to work in. In fact, nothing gives a TV professional more pleasure than to see someone they have worked with in the past go on to greater things.

Everyone at *Have I Got News For You* is delighted when ambitious strugglers on the lower rungs of the showbiz ladder receive a leg-up from having hosted the show. Some guest hosts sadly disappear without trace, others go on to do quite well. Here's where the more successful *HIGNFY* graduates have ended up. We can't claim all the credit but, as they say, every little helps.

Bruce Forsyth	*Strictly Come Dancing*
William Hague	Shadow Foreign Secretary
Des Lynam	*Countdown*
Boris Johnson	Shadow Spokesman on Higher Education (and all the totty he can handle)
Kirsty Young	*Desert Island Discs*
Andrew Marr	That Sunday morning thing
Dara O'Briain	*Mock the Week*
Charlotte Church	Friday night chatshow for drunks
Alexander Armstrong	Some more ads
Neil Kinnock	Taffy's Minicabs, Swansea
Robin Cook	Valhalla
Jimmy Carr	Everything

YAROO!

IAN HISLOP: 'Anyone for golf'?

PAUL MERTON: Is it, 'slow play on tennis court leads to office being built around Boris?'

YET MORE ODD ONES OUT

DARA O'BRIAIN (GUEST HOST): Which is the Odd One Out?

ADAM FAITH   SPIKE MILLIGAN

BENITO MUSSOLINI   MEL BLANC

JULIA HARTLEY-BREWER: Spike Milligan just had his headstone put in place, it's in Gaelic, but it says something like: 'I told you I was ill'. Famous last words.

IAN HISLOP: Because Adam Faith's, well he had very famous last words. He died in a hotel room in peculiar circumstances. Um, well I mean, I don't know quite how to describe it, really.

PAUL MERTON: Mel Blanc. He was the voice of all the Warner Brothers cartoons, and so surely it must have on his tombstone: 'That's all folks'. Adam Faith is the odd one out, because he hasn't got anything written on his, he said his last words rather than have them written on his tombstone.

DARA O'BRIAIN: Correct. The answer is they all wrote their own epitaphs, except Adam Faith, who's more remembered for his famous last words, which were, **'Channel 5 is all shit, isn't it? Christ, the crap they put on there. It's a waste of space.'** In 1945, Mussolini's body was strung up in front of a petrol station in Milan, and later buried beneath the words, **'Here lies one of the most intelligent animals ever to appear on the surface of the earth.'** Which was an improvement on: 'Diesel: 39p a litre'. Mussolini's granddaughter, Alessandra, is still a force in Italian politics. According to the *Independent*, **'There is no reason why a politician should not look like a porn star.'** Which is good news for Robert Kilroy Silk.

YOU PROBABLY THOUGHT WE'D RUN OUT OF MISSING WORDS

KIRSTY YOUNG (GUEST HOST): So we finish, as always, on the Missing Words round. This week's guest publication is *Jane Austen's Regency World*. 'It is a truth universally acknowledged that a single man in possession of a copy must be in want of a life.'

'PRAY PASS THE ▐██▌ MR BINGLEY?'

PAUL MERTON: Is it 'crack pipe'? This is from Jane Austen, isn't it? Duchy on the left-hand side?

IAN McMILLAN: Is it 'signals at green'?

JULIAN FELLOWES: I sort of nearly know this, it's driving me mad.

PAUL MERTON: Yes, I nearly don't know it, isn't it extraordinary.

KIRSTY YOUNG: The answer is 'Salmagundy'. According to *Jane Austen's Regency World*, **'Salmagundy is a cold dish containing ham, chicken, beetroot, pickles, eggs, anchovies and lemon.'** So, after passing the Salmagundy Mr Bingley, would you pray pass the bucket?

RONNIE CORBETT (GUEST HOST): So we finish, as always, on the Missing Words round. Or as the other Ronnie would put it, 'The Pissing Worms Round'. This week's guest publication is *Nursing Made Incredibly Easy*.

'WAIT A MINUTE, WHAT HAPPENED TO ▨ ?'

PAUL MERTON: 'What happened to the patient that was sitting by the open window on the fourth floor'?

TRACEY EMIN: 'What happened to the old lady that was chain smoking'?

RONNIE CORBETT: 'Hepatitis F' is the answer.

'I LOVE ▨ AND ▨, SAYS PRESCOTT?'

GERMAINE GREER: 'Jaguar and Jaguar'.

DANNY BAKER: 'Country and Western'.

PAUL MERTON: 'Simon and Garfunkel'.

DANNY BAKER: 'Ant and Dec'.

PAUL MERTON: 'Fish and Chips'.

DANNY BAKER: 'Sweet and sour'.

IAN HISLOP: 'Dick and Dom'.

PAUL MERTON: 'Bed and Breakfast'.

IAN HISLOP: 'I love hitting people with a left and a right'.

JEREMY CLARKSON (GUEST HOST): No, the answer is, 'I love coming to Tories' seats and roughing them up'.

' ███████ STUNNED BY VIBRATING PANTS?'

ROBERT LLEWELLYN: 'Concrete drill operator's wife.'

IAN HISLOP: 'SpongeBob'.

DAISY SAMPSON: It is 'Swansea's Asda'. A lady was wearing Ann Summers' leatherette vibrating pants. And she overdid it as she was doing her shopping in Asda in Swansea. And she had so many orgasms that she passed out, hit her head on a shelf. This is absolutely true, it was in the *Sun*.

PAUL MERTON: Believe me, if you live in Swansea it's worth doing.

DAISY SAMPSON: And she had to be rescued and her pants were still vibrating and she had passed out.

PAUL MERTON: Did she have to go into the 'six orgasms or less queue?' Other shoppers must think that she's really found a bargain. She's picking up a jar of mustard going, 'Yes, yes! Quick, buy the mustard, there's 21 pence off it. Yes! Have you got any family sized crisps!? Is it all right if I park my car here? Oh yes! Got any frozen peas? I'll defrost them myself.'

'DUCHESS IS ████, AS SHE SAMPLES DEVON CIDER?'

PETER SERAFINOWICZ: 'Fingered'.

PAUL MERTON: Yes.

WILLIAM HAGUE (GUEST HOST): The answer is, 'cheered'.

PAUL MERTON: It's the same thing in Devon.

WILLIAM HAGUE: Camilla attended the Devon Country and Livestock Show. The crowd cheered, although there was one embarrassing incident when the judge slapped her bottom and pinned a rosette behind her ear.

IAN HISLOP: Oh please.

'WI LADIES ACCUSED OF ████████?'

DAVID MITCHELL: Is this like sort of shooting-up on a bus, or smuggling smack and cannabis into the country?

IAN HISLOP: What, in jam?

DAVID MITCHELL: They do a fantastic quince and crack jam, yes. It's very very moreish.

DES LYNAM (GUEST HOST): You're almost there, the words actually are, 'nail varnish terror alert'. A coach party of WI members were stopped and searched by French police and sniffer dogs after a bomb scare. The French police were on the bus for an hour and only got off when the WI members threatened to strip off and pose for another calendar.

ZZZ ...

Did you drop off while doing the sudoku?

PRESCOTT IS FAT	BUSH IS STUPID	MENZIES IS OLD	CAMILLA ISN'T PRETTY	NORFOLK IS BACKWARD	BLAIR TELLS LIES	BROWN IS MISERLY	KILROY-SILK IS ORANGE	CAMERON IS POSH
BROWN IS MISERLY	CAMERON IS POSH	CAMILLA ISN'T PRETTY	MENZIES IS OLD	PRESCOTT IS FAT	KILROY-SILK IS ORANGE	BUSH IS STUPID	NORFOLK IS BACKWARD	BLAIR TELLS LIES
KILROY-SILK IS ORANGE	NORFOLK IS BACKWARD	BLAIR TELLS LIES	BROWN IS MISERLY	CAMERON IS POSH	BUSH IS STUPID	PRESCOTT IS FAT	MENZIES IS OLD	CAMILLA ISN'T PRETTY
MENZIES IS OLD	CAMILLA ISN'T PRETTY	NORFOLK IS BACKWARD	BLAIR TELLS LIES	BROWN IS MISERLY	PRESCOTT IS FAT	CAMERON IS POSH	BUSH IS STUPID	KILROY-SILK IS ORANGE
CAMERON IS POSH	KILROY-SILK IS ORANGE	PRESCOTT IS FAT	NORFOLK IS BACKWARD	(gun)	MENZIES IS OLD	BLAIR TELLS LIES	CAMILLA ISN'T PRETTY	BROWN IS MISERLY
BUSH IS STUPID	BLAIR TELLS LIES	BROWN IS MISERLY	CAMERON IS POSH	KILROY-SILK IS ORANGE	CAMILLA ISN'T PRETTY	NORFOLK IS BACKWARD	PRESCOTT IS FAT	MENZIES IS OLD
BLAIR TELLS LIES	BROWN IS MISERLY	BUSH IS STUPID	KILROY-SILK IS ORANGE	CAMILLA ISN'T PRETTY	NORFOLK IS BACKWARD	MENZIES IS OLD	CAMERON IS POSH	PRESCOTT IS FAT
NORFOLK IS BACKWARD	MENZIES IS OLD	KILROY-SILK IS ORANGE	PRESCOTT IS FAT	BLAIR TELLS LIES	CAMERON IS POSH	CAMILLA ISN'T PRETTY	BROWN IS MISERLY	BUSH IS STUPID
CAMILLA ISN'T PRETTY	PRESCOTT IS FAT	CAMERON IS POSH	BUSH IS STUPID	MENZIES IS OLD	BROWN IS MISERLY	KILROY-SILK IS ORANGE	BLAIR TELLS LIES	NORFOLK IS BACKWARD

ERRATUM

Due to a printing error, the gun, which was meant to be one of the hidden objects in the Heraldic Coat-of-Arms on page 56, did not appear in its intended position. It was wrongly inserted into the Sudoku solution instead.

We apologize for any inconvenience this oversight may have caused our readers, and hope that your enjoyment of both puzzles has not been impaired.

ACKNOWLEDGMENTS

THE AUTHORS

Ged Parsons has been a Programme Associate on HIGNFY since 1997. He prides himself on creating jokes that fit precisely to whatever format he is currently

John Ryan has worked on HIGNFY since the very first episode. All right, he started by making the coffees, but it all counts, doesn't it?

Richard Wilson produced HIGNFY for ten years. As editor, his particular skill is in poof-reading.

Thanks to all the Programme Associates (see Credits). Recent regulars include: Mark Burton, Rob Colley, Dan Gaster, Ged Parsons, Pete Sinclair and Colin Swash. These are the writers who make the show what it is today – over-staffed, expensive and slow to produce.

Thanks also to Deirdre Heaney, and Sarah Murcoch.

PICTURE CREDITS